Introduction:
Mindset, Motivation and Money

Let me ask you a question...

Why do you want an e-commerce store?

No seriously, take a moment and honestly answer that question.

And then answer these questions:

☐ Do you want an e-commerce store because you're looking for a way to make money online?

☐ Do you want a store because you're looking for a way to turn your passions and hobbies into money in the bank?

☐ Do you want a store as a supplement to what you're already doing? For example, maybe you already have a dog training site, and now you'd like to create another revenue stream on the site by selling physical products.

☐ Do you already make goods, and you're looking for an outlet to sell them?

☐ Did you read about someone else having big success with an online store, and that made you daydream about having your own uber-successful store?

☐ Does it look like an easy way to make money to you?

☐ Do you want a store because it seems like a good way to help your niche market?

- [ ] Do you want a store because you like the idea of owning something? In other words, do you imagine putting "CEO and store owner" on a business card and impressing friends and strangers alike?
- [ ] Do you want a store because your brother / sister / friend / colleague said they were starting a store, and your ultra-competitive nature kicked in so you wanted a store too?

- [ ] Do you want a store because your current online marketing gig isn't working out, and you're pretty sure a store would be a much better business for you?

- [ ] Do you want a store because you tend to chase bright and shiny things, and this seems awfully bright and shiny today?

Those are just a few questions to get you brainstorming.

But basically, you need to be honest about WHY you want to start up an ecommerce store.

The reason you need to be honest about the "why" is because your answer can make or break your success.

Here's the thing...

There are a lot of people who get into ecommerce for all the wrong reasons. And when that happens, they fail. Big time.

You see, starting up an ecommerce store isn't a decision you should make lightly.

This isn't a decision like, *"What should I have for dinner tonight?"* or *"Should I do laundry or just buy more socks?"*

This is a big decision, one that is going to affect you every day for as long as you own this store. And if you don't have a fire in your belly about your store, then you're going to give up a few months down the road.

Because you know what?

Not every day as a store owner is all rainbows and puppies.

And you may not be making profits right out of the gate.

Sure, some days you're going to be so excited about your store that you're going to fly out of bed in the morning because you're so eager to get to work on it.

But then there are going to be those days when things are hard. You're frustrated. Seems like things are going wrong.

If you aren't building an e-commerce store for the right reasons, those are the days you're going to toss in the towel.

Let me give you a heads-up...

If your #1 sole and overriding reason to set up an e-commerce store is to make money – or you're doing it for ego reasons -- then I'm betting you're going to quit this gig just a few months down the road!
Because working on your store every day, every week, every month and every year is going to get old really fast if money is your ONLY reason for doing it.

Sure, making money is a big reason. I get it. You need to make a living.

But it shouldn't be your only reason.

There needs to be something else driving your passion.

You need to be excited about your niche. You need to genuinely care about your customers and want what is best for them.

Because it's this deep-seated enthusiasm and care that is going to propel you to keep going even when things get tough.

Do you have it? Is there a fire in your belly? Are you excited to keep reading even though I just rained on the ecommerce parade with a cold dose of reality?

If so, then those are very good signs.

If you're still feeling excited, then I'm thinking you've got what it takes to be a success. **And you are reading the book that's going to help make it happen.**

Over the next several dozen pages you're going to discover the exact step-by-step strategy for setting up and running your own successful e-commerce store, including:

☐ The right way to choose a niche and product line.

☐ How to set up a platform that simplifies e-commerce.

☐ Where to get your products.

☐ How to bring in massive amounts of targeted traffic.

And much, much more.

Let's jump in...

"The <u>Niche</u> Is The Thing That Catches The Profits... And Secures The Bling!"

At this point we've determined that you have the right mindset and motivation to start and run an ecommerce store.

So, the next thing you need to do is pick a niche and product line.

This step is hugely important.

Because if you go running after a niche full of deadbeats and tire-kickers, your dreams are going to go up in smoke. If you pick a profitable niche but you screw up and choose the wrong product line, you're going to waste a lot of time and money getting your business back on track.

So here's the deal...

You want to do it right the first time.

Now, when it comes to picking your niche, you have two goals:

1. **You need to pick something that interests you.** Remember, you're going to be working in this niche every day for years – if you're lukewarm about it before you even get started, then you're going to hate it in six months from now.

2. **You need to be sure the niche is profitable.** No amount of passion can make a niche profitable if no one is buying what you're selling. That's why we're going to make sure your passion can generate profits.

The good news is that it's entirely possible to turn a passion into profits.

Take a look at these examples and feel inspired:

Here's a store from an entrepreneur who took a strong brand and a niche idea, and turned it into a million-dollar store in less than a year: **http://www.beardbrand.com**

Here's another example of a small niche idea (that started out with leggings) that took off like crazy and turned into a million-dollar venture: **https://blackmilkclothing.com**

Here's someone who took a love for temporary tattoos and turned it into a thriving store that sells millions of these tattoos: **https://tattly.com**

Or how about the guy who has a million-dollar business selling nothing but black socks with a unique "sock scription" business model? His website is, you guessed it: **www.blacksocks.com**

Those are just a few examples. Just think of your favorite niche, and you'll quickly find online stores that started as a dream for someone and turned into a profitable reality.

You'll find people selling most everything under the sun, from jewelry to handmade greeting cards to caskets for pets to clothing to sports memorabilia to electronics to... well, I could go on and on.

If there is a market for an idea, then someone out there is probably making a lot money with it – and you can too.

TIP: Take note that several of the stores mentioned above are very nitrified and specific (like black socks or temporary tattoos). As we walk through the following steps of picking a niche and product line, you too will want to seek out something narrow. That's because it's easier to set up, promote, and run a successful niche business that's narrower rather than broader.

We'll talk about this in a bit more detail shortly. *So, let's get brainstorming on possible markets, and then take a look at whether those possible markets are profitable...*

Uncovering Passions For Profit

First things first – let's figure out what sorts of topics are going to hold your interest.

We'll do this in two steps.

First, you'll draw up a big list of potential markets and niches.

Then you'll figure out which ones interest you the most.

So, let's start by brainstorming niches.

In order to do this step, ask yourself these questions:

☐ What are you really good at?

☐ What are your hobbies?

☐ What are your problems?

☐ What types of things do you like to read?

☐ What sort of sites do you have bookmarked on your computer?

☐ What sort of apps do you have on your phone?

☐ What do you like to watch on TV?

☐ What are your favorite topics of conversation?

☐ What sort of educational or hobby classes would you be interested in taking?

☐ On what topics do people marvel at your knowledge?

And I'd also add - What topics have you loved for years *(and that you're likely to be interested in for years to come)?*

Now list all the other topics you can think of that interest you.

Okay, so now that you've done some initial brainstorming, I want you to go through the following list and pick out any of these topics that also interest you:

☐ Hiking and camping.

☐ Medical problems, including physical and mental health issues, as well as chronic illness.

☐ Caring for elderly parents.

☐ Antiques, collectibles, jewelry.

☐ Babies, children, family.

☐ Relationships and marriage.

☐ Sports hobbies, including golf, archery, fishing, bowling, etc.

☐ Other hobbies, such as car restoration, cooking, dining out, etc.

☐ Fashion and beauty.

☐ Anti-aging.

☐ Making money, including marketing, and entrepreneurialism.

☐ General finances, including investing/debt management.

☐ Retirement, financial security/becoming an ex-pat.

☐ Traveling, backpacking the EU to living an RV lifestyle.

☐ Home remodeling and home improvement.

☐ Diets, including vegetarianism, raw food diets, etc.

☐ Weight loss.

☐ Bodybuilding.

☐ Motivation.

☐ Productivity and time management.

☐ Other self-help (e.g., public speaking, feeling more confident, finding happiness, etc.).

☐ Grief and mourning.

☐ Bad habits, such as stopping smoking.

☐ Pets and animals.

☐ Career and job.

☐ Music, including learning an instrument or learning how to sing.

☐ Languages (e.g., learn French).

☐ Self-defense.

☐ Home security.

☐ Computer security.

☐ Stress relief, such as meditation and yoga.

☐ Weddings.

You'll note that many of these are very broad.

What you want to do is figure out what sub-topics/niches within these broad markets most interest you.

For example, maybe you have an interest in bodybuilding, and perhaps you've even taken up the hobby yourself. You might find a niche from your perspective, such as bodybuilding for people over 40. Or you might look at a specific problem, such as people who travel a lot and don't always have access to weights, in which case you'd look at portable solutions like bands.

Another example: you care for your elderly parents, and you've noticed that bath time is an especially dangerous time for them. So, you might focus on selling bathing mobility aids and safety devices, such as grab handles, bath benches, walk-in bath tubs, showers that accommodate wheel chairs, and similar items.

The point is, spend some time right now narrowing down your potential markets to a specific niche or problem.

And then have a look-see at the next step...

Where Interest Intersects With Income

Now that we know what interests you, we need to find the niches (and product lines) that are going to put money in your pocket.

In other words, it's time for some market research.

Now there are two main methods for conducting market research, and a good strategy will incorporate both of them:

1. **Find out what your market is already buying.** Big hint: if they're already buying something similar, then that's a big green flag telling you that they'll buy it from you too (if you carve yourself out a piece of a niche).

2. **Find out what your market wants.** In other words, find out what they're talking about in the niche, and ask them what they want and need.

Heads up...

Sometimes marketers figure it's easier to skip the first step and just ask the market what they want.

But here's the thing... What your market SAY they want and what they'll actually buy can be two different things. So that's why you want to see what people are actually actively buying today because that's a good predictor of what they'll buy tomorrow.

And then you can survey the market for two reasons:

1. **To confirm your research.** If your market is telling you they want something AND you see evidence that they're already buying it, that's excellent! You got a profitable product line on your hands.

2. **To discover ways to improve on what the competition is doing** (such as designing a unique selling proposition that will hook your market).

Okay, so let's go through these two steps of finding out what people are buying, and finding out what they say they want...

Follow the Money: There are two ways to follow the money when it comes to your market research:

1. Find out where your prospective customers are laying down their money. In other words, what are they buying?

2. Find out where your prospective customers are laying down money for advertising, because savvy marketers don't investment endless sums of money in unprofitable product lines.

Here's how to figure out what your market is buying...

Search marketplaces. Simply enter your niche keywords into top marketplaces, and see which products are selling well.

For example, if you're looking at organic rose gardening, then you'd search the various marketplaces using the keywords ... (wait for it)... "organic rose gardening."

__TIP:__ Keep your keywords broad for now, as it will help you uncover products you may have never considered before.

You can search marketplaces such as:

☐ Amazon.com
☐ Etsy.com.
☐ CafePress.com
☐ Zazzle.com
☐ Bonanza.com
☐ eBay.com

Take note that several of these marketplaces give you an indication of what's selling well.

For example, Amazon lists products according to their ranking in the marketplace, so it's easy for you to pick out the top sellers in a niche.

__TIP:__ Not only should you look for bestsellers, but also look for similar products which are all selling well. This shows you that a bestselling product isn't a fluke. Instead, it shows consistency since similar products are selling well too.

Search Google. Now go search for your niche keywords in Google or Bing.

Take note of the following:

1. What are the top sites in your niche selling? If several sites in your niche are selling similar products, that's a good sign that the product is popular.

2. What are the top sites in your niche advertising? In some cases, a top site might not directly sell their own products. Instead, they may accept advertisers. Take note of what these

advertisers are promoting – if you see similar ads across sites, that's a sign that a product is in demand.

3. What do you see being advertised in the sponsored results? You'll find these sponsored (paid) ads next to the organic ads in Google or Bing. If you see similar products being advertised across ads, that's a sign that it's something popular in your niche.

Check out print publications. Here's what you're looking for:

1.See what niche catalogs are selling. In particular, pay attention to what is promoted on the front and back covers. These are the big items that tend to be popular, and those who print catalogs do a lot of research and testing to determine which items to put on the front and back covers.

For example, if you're looking to sell gardening supplies, then check out what the top gardening supply catalogs are positioning as their big sellers.

2.See what's being advertised in niche magazines. Popular magazines (with large circulation numbers) charge a lot to advertise, so advertisers pick their products and offers carefully. Check out the ads scattered through these magazines, as well as the classified ads in the back (where applicable).

Next...

Find Out What Your Market Wants

This is the part where you eavesdrop on your market, do a little investigative work to figure out what your market wants, and outright ask them what they want.

Again, take note that you shouldn't use this method in insolation, as what people say and what they do can be two different things.

Walk through these three steps:

Eavesdrop on your market. In other words, simply spend some time listening to your market talk amongst themselves, which can be very revealing.

You can find these discussions in the following places:

☐ On niche blogs (check the comments).
☐ In communities, such as Facebook groups or forums.
☐ In product reviews on sites like Amazon.

TIP: Check the discussions on product review sites to see what people are saying about products in your niche.

Use keyword tools. The next step is to enter your niche keywords into a tool such as **Keyword Atlas**.
For discount go to **https://paykstrt.com/13994/138738**

Then pay particular attention to the keywords that revolve around specific products and product reviews.

For example, if you've decided to sell shoes to marathon runners, then take note of what types of shoes are getting a lot of searches, which ones have plenty of searches for product reviews, and which types of shoes people are looking to outright buy.

(E.G., "buy [brand name] running shoe" or "[brand name] running shoe free shipping)

Survey your market. Finally, you can ask your market what they want. One way to do this is by using a tool like SurveyMonkey.com. Another way is to simply open the discussion on a big platform, like in a social media group, in a sort of focus group. Or, preferably, you can do both.

Either way, don't constrain answers to fit into some narrow category by using multiple choice questions. Instead, use at least some open-ended questions to get answers that you may not have even thought to include.

Research Complete: Now What?

At this point, you've figured out what interests you. You've taken the steps to determine if a niche is profitable. And in the process, you've also seen, specifically, which products get your prospective customers' hearts racing.

Now if you have several niches in mind, you need to narrow it down.

Ask yourself the following questions (and be prepared to possibly do a little more research in order to answer them):

Which niches are evergreen?

To help you figure out the answer to this question, you can use a tool such as **Google Trends**, which will show you if a niche has enduring popularity. **https://www.google.com/trends/**

Unless you're a seasoned marketer who can spot new markets/trends, it's better to stick with niches that have a history of being popular (*meaning they are likely to continue to grow in popularity over time*).

Which niches appear to be the most profitable?

Check your research, and look to see whether an overall market has a lot of competition. If there are a lot of marketers selling a lot of products, <u>consider that a good sign!</u>

Of course, you don't want to compete with everyone, which brings us to the next point...

Where can you carve out a niche?

It's okay to have competition – it will make you stronger and better. And it's a sign of a healthy market.

But what you want to do is carve out a smaller niche so that you can dominate it. Ask yourself if you see any gaps in the market.

Let me give you an example...
Remember when cell phones first started exploding in popularity? And then the smart phones came along, and everyone was racing to sell the most sophisticated phones on the planet?
Well, that is except for one company: **Jitterbug.**

This company focused on selling **"dumb" phones** with big buttons to senior citizens. These phones were for the technophobes who wanted to use their phones to make calls (yeah, I know... weird!). And the company did really well, because they found a gap in the market and dominated their niche.

So again, ask yourself where the gaps are in your market.

Is there an under-served niche where there is a demand, but the companies aren't all that great at supplying that demand?

That's where you can step in.

Which niches appeal to you the most?

With all else being equal in terms of profit potential and so on, the last question you need to ask yourself is which niche most interests you? Because again, you're going to be working in this niche every day for quite some time to come, so you need to make sure it's something you'll enjoy.

Consider these questions carefully, select the niche and product line that is most profitable while still being of interest to you, and then let's move onto the next exciting step...

Platform + Performance = Profits

There's a reason why smart builders spend a lot of time consulting with architects before they start laying bricks. And that reason is because if the foundation of their building isn't stable, the whole darn building is going to fall down like a house of cards.

Guess what?

Your ecommerce store is the same way. If you pick an unstable or unsecure platform, your whole business is going to collapse beneath the weight of this bad decision. Or even if that sort of catastrophe doesn't happen, at the very least you'll lose time and money if you have to start over later with a different platform.

Point is, it's a good idea to do a little researching and comparing upfront to save yourself time, money and heartache down the road.

And that's what this chapter will help you do.

Now if you just drop a search into Google to look for ecommerce platforms, you'll quickly discover that there are dozens if not hundreds of solutions. These solutions include open-source standalone platforms, as well as third-party platforms that host your store and take care of a lot of the details for you.

Truth is, it's overwhelming to even start contemplating digging through all of these solutions and figuring out which ones are legit. And that's why we're going to give you a short list of the BEST platforms out there. These are the platforms that we've reviewed, tested and use ourselves to run our own stores. So all you have to do is compare them to see which one is right for you.

TIP: Of course one option is to build your own store from the group up by hiring a team of developers. But you know what? It's a very expensive option, and there are going to be concerns about whether your platform can keep your customers' data safe. It's much easier to take advantage of any number of big, secure solutions that others have spent millions to develop. That's what you'll find in this list below.

Take a look at these options...

WordPress + WooCommerce

WordPress is a popular content management system (CMS), and WooCommerce is a robust plugin you can use to turn your WordPress site into an e-commerce platform where you sell your own products.

Here are the advantages of using WordPress + WooCommerce:

☐ It's a stable, secure platform. WordPress was originally developed in 2001, and it's been constantly updated and improved every year since by a large number of developers. The WooCommerce plugin was first developed in 2011, and today it boasts millions of downloads and is one of the top e-commerce platforms.

☐ You're in control. It's your store, it's your domain, it's your web hosting. You have complete control over how you run your store (within the terms of service of your web host, of course).

☐ You don't pay per-transaction fees to the platform. Sure, like any store, you'll have per-transaction fees from your payment processor. But since you own the store and platform, you do NOT have to pay per-transaction fees to a third-party platform.

☐ WordPress and WooCommerce are user-friendly. They both have a lot of online documentation, and you can find peer support communities.

☐ WooCommerce is flexible, extendable and adaptable. You can get plugins to add functionality, or let a developer customize the open-source code. You can also choose from many WordPress themes (both free and paid) to create a design that best fits your store.

Sounds good, right? Before you make a decision, you'll want to check out these disadvantages:

 WooCommerce paid extensions can add up. The WordPress platform is free, and the basic WooCommerce plugin is free. However, you will likely need to purchase a few plugins in order to get the functionality you want. So you need to be sure you research the core features and plugins in depth so that you can properly estimate your total cost.

 The tech stuff is up to you. While you're in complete control of your site (which is good), you're also completely responsible for the technical aspects of your site.

For example: if something "breaks" (like an extension breaks during a WordPress update), you'll need to scramble and put in a temporary fix while you wait for the developer to get you a permanent fix.

Another example: If your server goes down, that is your responsibility (or your web host's) to get it back.

 Potentially slow loading times. If you have a lot of variations of a product, you may find that your storefront loads slowly – and that's not good for business.

 There is no telephone support. WooCommerce offers support through a help desk only. There are third-party businesses that will offer support through the phone, but these are not affiliated with WooCommerce. You can also find peer-supported forums to get help.

To learn more about the WordPress platform, go to www.wordpress.org.

Or try webwave website and text creator using AI go to
https://webwave.ro/ref/7443532957

To learn more about WooCommerce, go to **https://woocommerce.com**

Or try webwave website and text creator using AI go to
https://webwave.ro/ref/7443532957

Now let's look at another popular option...

Shopify

Shopify started in 2006 when its developers were looking for a robust, secure way to sell their own snowboards. They quickly realized they had developed a platform that others would want, so they offered to host other peoples' stores on their platform.

Today Shopify is one of the most popular third-party e-commerce platforms. It's hosted hundreds of thousands of stores and done tens of billions of dollars in sales.

Let's take a look at the pros and cons of this third-party platform...

Here are the advantages of using Shopify:

◻ It's secure. This platform has been around since 2006, and it's being constantly updated to ensure it is secure.

◻ It's flexible and scalable. You can choose from a tiered pricing plan to pick the level that best fits your needs, and then upgrade as your business grows.

◻ It's customizable. Shopify includes both free and paid themes to create a beautiful storefront, plus you can install apps to get more functionality.

◻ Good customer support. Not only does Shopify have extensive documentation, but they also offer telephone support.

◌ You're in control. You're in complete control of your store, but Shopify hosts it for you and ensures it's secure. This means you can do important tasks such as build an email list of both prospects and customers.

And here are the disadvantages of using Shopify:

◌ Pricing uncertainty. Shopify's tiered pricing is straightforward, as you pay a per-month fee. However, in order to determine your final cost, you're going to need to know what all apps you plan on installing. Some are free, some are paid, and some require a per-transaction fee.

◌ Learning curve. Any platform is going to have a learning curve. While Shopify is overall straightforward, some users may have troubles due to non-intuitive labeling. Still, no worries: you don't need to be developer to set it up.

◌ Checkout cannot be customized. The reason for this is because Shopify is PCI compliant, which is a good thing – it means they're keeping your customers' credit card data safe. But on the other hand, you don't have much leeway with the looks of the order form, which may be a disadvantage if you'd like to create a little more continuity between your store and the checkout process.

Shopify + Dropshipping

With Shopify, you can easily set up a store selling your own products. However, for those who don't have their own products, another option is to set up a dropshipping business model. An easy way to do this is by using AliExpress.com, which offers you thousands of products across many different categories.

NOTE: While AliExpress is a trusted dropshipping solution that gives you the potential for good profit margins, it's not without its issues. Delivery times can be lengthy since products are coming from Asia. What's more, customer service/communication is often lacking with this company.

What makes this model so attractive is that you can use the **Dropified** or go to **https://dropified.com?fpr=marian48** app to find products on AliExpress and load them to your store fairly fast. Instead of adding products manually (which can be very tedious and time-consuming), you can drag and drop them into the app and let the software do it for you.

This is a great option for someone who wants a store, but doesn't want the traditional hassles of stocking inventory and shipping products.

Here's the next platform for you to consider...

Amazon

Amazon doesn't need any introduction, as it's been around since the mid 1990s, and offering its platform to sellers since 2000. Let's take a look at the pros and cons of selling on Amazon...

Here are the advantages of using Amazon's platform:

◻ Credibility and trust. You're using Amazon's trusted brand to help you sell your own products, which is a big benefit. You're likely to see bigger conversions over setting up your own store.

◻ Built-in traffic. Amazon works hard to market your products, including recommending your products to your prospects both on their website as well as through email.

- ☐ Security. Amazon is known for having a secure, PCI-compliant platform, and you can take advantage of this when you set up your store with them.

- ☐ You can use FBA (fulfillment by Amazon). This feature lets you ship your merchandise to Amazon, who then will take care of everything for a fee (including fulfillment, returns and customer service issues).

- ☐ Amazon takes care of the details, such as collecting taxes. This simplifies selling, since you don't need to know the tax laws for every state.

Here are the disadvantages of using Amazon's platform:

☐ It's not on your site. You don't have the control as you do when you set up a store on your own domain with your own web hosting. And that means you also don't get to capture your prospects' addresses and other information. And in cases where you receive the customers' contact information, it is against Amazon's terms of service to market to them.

☐ Fees can be high. Fees vary depending on whether you're taking care of fulfillment yourself or paying Amazon to do it, so be sure to make comparisons carefully. If you sell as a professional on Amazon, you'll pay a per-month fee plus variable referral and closing fees. See Amazon's pricing page for more information

https://sell.amazon.com/

> NOTE: When considering fees, also consider that you will likely have lower marketing costs. So while fees may be higher, possibly those fees could be offset by lowered costs.

❒ Direct competition. When you use Amazon, you'll have other people on the same platform who are selling the exact same thing, which often results in people slashing their prices to compete. Plus if Amazon ends up selling your product, then you'll be in direct competition with them too.

To learn more about Amazon's selling platform: go to https://promotelabs.com/blog/amazon-payments-payment-processor-review/

And now let's look at the next platform option...

Etsy

If you're interested in selling your own handmade arts and crafts, then Etsy is a good option. That's because people who shop on Etsy are looking for and expect to find handmade goods. So let's take a look at the pros and cons of this platform...

Here are the advantages of selling on Etsy:

❒ Setting up your store is easy. While it may be a little time- consuming to set up a lot of listings, the process itself is intuitive and easy.

❒ Etsy sends you some traffic. That's because Etsy will refer prospects to your listings via recommendations.

❒ Etsy is a trusted brand. And that means you're likely to see higher conversions by putting your crafts on Etsy versus putting the on your own site. (But of course you'd need to test this to determine if it's true and/or if it's significant.)

Here are the disadvantages of selling on Etsy:

❒ You have direct competition on the platform. Even if you're selling something completely original, there's a good chance that a copycat will pop up soon and cut into your profits.

Fees on low-cost products. If you're selling low-priced items, the per-listing and per-sale transaction fees will cut into your profits. That's because the listing fee is a flat 20 cents per item, regardless of how much the item costs, plus a 3.5% transaction fee on sales plus payment processor fees. Be sure to price accordingly, or stick to "premium" (higher priced) items with bigger profit margins.

 You can lose your own sense of branding. While you do get the benefits of using Etsy's trusted brand, this can also be a negative when you're trying to stand out from the crowd. When people share where they bought your handmade item, they're not going to name you (the artist or handcrafter) by name – instead, they're going to say they got it from Etsy.

You can learn more about this platform by going to:

https://www.etsy.com/sell or go to for free listing:

https://etsy.me/3iAjVEv

eBay

This platform is another one that's been around for a long time – since 1995 – so it's trusted by both sellers and buyers alike. Let's take a look at the pros and cons of selling your goods on eBay...

Here are the advantages of selling on eBay:

 You can sell both used and new merchandise. And you can sell most anything, from handmade items to low-priced used goods to high-end merchandise.

 Built-in traffic. People who visit eBay are buyers, and you're likely to get plenty of this warm traffic to your listings if you include the right keywords in the title and descriptions.

- eBay is a trusted brand. And once again, that means (potentially) higher conversions when you sell on this platform versus on your own site, but of course you'd need to test to see if that's the case.

- Setting up a store and listings are easy. There are plenty of services that simplify the process, such as templates to create a beautiful listing, and bulk-listing services to make the process go more quickly.

- You can use the valet service. This service lets you ship your items (for free) to professional sellers, who'll then take care of everything else, including listing the item, payment processing, and fulfillment. In return for this service, you'll earn from 25% to 80% of the item's selling price. Learn more at http://www.ebay.com/s/valet.

Here are the disadvantages of selling on eBay:

- You have plenty of direct competition on the site. This alone often drives prices down. And since people come to eBay looking for bargains, it's hard to compete in this marketplace if your prices are higher than everyone else's prices.

- Fees can be high, depending on what you're selling. You'll pay insertion fees, final value fees, store fees, payment processor fees, and (optionally) advanced listing fees.

Note: you get 50 insertion-fee-free listings for certain types of merchandise per month if you're a basic seller, and more if you have a store. See

http://pages.ebay.com/help/sell/insertion-fee.html#free for more details.

- Your payment options are limited. Since PayPal is owned by eBay, that's the payment processor of choice for this platform. You can also accept payment through your own merchant account. Most other payment options – even checks sent by mail – are limited or restricted in some way. See eBay's terms for complete details to see if your payment option is accepted.

To learn more about selling on eBay, go to http://www.ebay.com/sl/sell.

So which platform is right for you?

Obviously, this is a decision that you're going to need to make based on your own needs, goals, budget, and preferences. Here are the issues to take into consideration:

☐ What sort of products are you selling? Different platforms have different fees, depending on what you're selling, so you'll need to take that into consideration when determining cost. You'll also need to check the terms of service on each site to be sure that the platform accepts your type of product. If you're selling something prohibited by other sites (such as firearms), then you'll need to consider selling on your own site (such as by using WordPress + WooCommerce).

☐ What is your level of technical expertise? If you have low levels of technical expertise and/or you don't intend to outsource the development of your site, then you'll need to stick with third-party, hosted platforms (rather than self-hosted options like WordPress). All you do is pay a monthly fee, and it's headache free.

☐ Do you intend to stock and fulfill merchandise? If you don't carry inventory, then a dropshipping model is a good option (think Shopify plus the Shopified App and AliExpress), or you can use a service such as eBay's valet service or Fulfillment by Amazon.

What is your marketing plan? It's a good idea to market your store aggressively in order to grow it as quickly as possible. However, some platforms – such as eBay, Etsy and Amazon – help you with marketing, and you get the benefit of their branding to boost conversions.

 How fast do you expect to grow? You need to be sure you pick a platform that can grow with you. Consider not only how many products you intend to list, but also what sort of volume you plan on doing. Some options, such as Shopify, let you start with a smaller plan and then upgrade as your business grows.

 What is your budget? Obviously, this is going to have an impact on your decision. But keep in mind, you don't want to go for an unsuitable option just because it's cheaper, otherwise you may need to start over later at a great cost of time and money.

So go ahead and consider these questions carefully, and then visit each site listed above to really compare your options. You'll also want to check out the bonus resource document for more tools.

Choose the one that's right for you, and then move onto the next step...

Turning Tire-Kicking Browsers Into Big-Spending Buyers

At this point you've picked a niche, picked a product line, and picked a platform. Your next step is to set up your store and start creating your listings so you can convert browsers into buyers.

But hold up there for a moment...

A lot of store owners do this step as quickly as possible. They are so anxious to get going that they slap some pretty weak descriptions and product photos up. And then they pay dearly for it later when sales are running as slow as an elderly snail. Except they don't realize that their listings are the source of slow sales.

So let me be really clear with you here...

Your product listings can make or break the success of your store, no matter what platform you're using. Yes, the listings matter THAT much. And that's why it's so important that you take your time to create your listings the right way.

Take a look at these important factors...

Creating Titles

One of the most important parts of your listing is your title. Here are two reasons why:

  1. Your title needs to be compelling enough to grab attention. If your prospects say "meh" to themselves after reading your product title, you can bet they won't be clicking on it. And there goes the sale.

2. Your title may help funnel traffic to your listing. This is particularly true on platforms like eBay, where the default search function is to search titles for keywords.

So what you need to do is create a sizzling listing title that captures attention and gets clicks.

Here's how...

Step 1: Consider Your Keywords

First, determine if you're going to include keywords in your title. You can determine these words in two ways:

☐ Use keyword tools. These tools (such as WordRecon) generally show you what types of searches people are inputting into the search engines. This will help you attract search engine traffic as well as internal traffic from platforms such as eBay.

☐ Do a little brainstorming. In other words, spend some time figuring out what sorts of words people might type into a search box to find your item.

For example, let's suppose you have a dog collar. Ask yourself: What similar words may people use in lieu of "dog" when searching for a collar? Most likely, someone might search for "puppy," and in rare instances they'd search for "canine." Generally, using "dog" would be sufficient, though you should add "puppy" if the collar is indeed suitable for puppies. Next...

Step 2: Describe Your Item Succinctly

Now you need to determine the most important aspects of your product. You can help determine these by asking yourself the following questions.

Take note that not all questions will be applicable to every product:

- What is the product?
- Who is it for?
- What does the product do?
- What color is it?
- What is it made out of?
- How big is it?
- When was it made?
- Who made it/brand name?
- Where was it made?
- Is it rare in some way?
- Is it new or used?
- Is it an antique or collectible?

For example, let's go back to the example of selling something as simple as a new dog collar.

Your prospects will be interested in the following:

- What is the product? Dog collar (and puppy collar, if applicable).

- Who is it for? Dogs, yes... big dogs? Small dogs? Sled dogs?

- What does the product do? This is important if it's a special kind of collar, like a choke collar.

- What color is it? Black, brown, red, purple paisley, red polka dots, etc.?

- What is it made out of? For example: leather? Nylon? Something else?

- How big is it? Here you might list the length and width of the collar, OR what breeds it fits. Or if you have a variety of sizes, you can leave this out of the title and provide the options in the description.

- Who made it? Some people may be interested in the brand name.

Since this is a new collar, generally the other questions are irrelevant. So now you might have something descriptive such as:

"Small black leather dog collar"

Not bad. It's descriptive, but not exciting. So let's polish that up…

Step 3: Polish Up Your Description

Your last step is to put a little spit and polish on your description so that it captures attention. The descriptive title is going to bring the traffic and help qualify it, but it's the little sizzle in the title that's going to get the clicks.

Now in most cases you don't have a lot of room to add this sizzle – you may only have two or three words. So make 'em count.

One way to add this sizzle is to add a benefit into the title. This could be a benefit of the product itself, or a benefit related to the ordering or shipping process.

Here are examples:

- Very stylish small black leather dog collar
- Small black leather dog collar – cute!
- Small black leather dog collar (fast shipping)
- Small black leather dog collar (free shipping)
- Your dog will turn heads with this black leather dog collar
- Surprisingly affordable small black leather dog collar
- Small black leather dog collar (high quality at a low price)
- Small, stylish black leather collar – will last for 20 years
- Best small black leather dog collar online – check it out!
- Fancy small black leather dog collar
- Amazingly soft/durable black leather collar for small dogs
- The #1 toughest black leather dog collar for small dogs

The #1 choice black leather collar for small dogs

Again, those are just examples pertaining to a dog collar. You need to get creative and polish up whatever product title you're creating by inserting a benefit or emotionally laden words.

Ideally, you should test different titles to see which ones get the clicks and conversions.

Next...

Crafting Sales Descriptions

Another very important factor in your success is to create a compelling sales description for every product you list.

Heads up...

If you're using a dropshipping service like AliExpress, rewrite the descriptions. That's because most of their descriptions are awful and won't generate sales. Plus writing your own descriptions will help you stand out.

So, what you need to do is start with the list of questions above, which covers the basics of your product. Then ask these questions:

 What are the features of the product? These are the actual parts of a product. For example, a feature of a dog collar is that it's made of nylon.

 What are the benefits of the product? This is what the features of a product do for the customer. List as many of these benefits as you can think of.

For example, while a feature of a dog collar is that it's made of nylon, the benefits of nylon include quick drying and ease- of-cleaning. This is a great advantage for dogs who like to go swimming. Nylon is also lightweight for small dogs, and durable for rough and tumble wear.

⬜ Who is the product most suited for? When applicable, list who would benefit the most from this product.

In the nylon dog collar example, we could say the collar is suitable for any dog, but the quick-drying collar is especially good for dogs who like to swim, such as labs.

⬜ What are the potential flaws of the product? And how can you rationalize and overcome these flaws? In other words, raise and handle potential objections to help people make the buying decision.

For example, perhaps one flaw of the collar is that it only comes in bright green, bright red and bright orange. You can turn this perceived liability into an asset by saying that these bright colors put your dog's safety first.

⬜ Does the product require any special care? For example, if you're selling clothing, you would note if it's dry clean only.

⬜ What are the product's measurements and size? This includes length, height and even weight.

NOTE: Be sure to list product measurements on clothing even if you've listed the size.

⬜ How is this product different from other products on the market? In other words, why should people buy this particular product? What makes it better than the competition?

Let's go back to the dog collar example. Perhaps it has a "quick-release buckle" that ensures a sporting dog never strangles himself when he gets snagged by a tree branch.

☐ Are there any discounts or freebies available? This includes things like free shipping, as well as any discounts that may be available.

☐ Are there any bonuses included? For example, if you're selling shoes, perhaps you toss in an extra pair of laces or even some shoe polish for free.

☐ Does the product come with any sort of guarantee? If so, what are the terms of this guarantee? Do customers need to pay return shipping? What is the length of the guarantee? Is it a money-back guarantee, or do you only offer product replacement?

☐ Is there anything else the prospect should know that will help them make the buying decision? Go ahead and list everything that comes to mind, even if it seems trivial.

Now that you've answered all these questions, you can write your product description and incorporate as many relevant details as possible. Be sure to focus on the benefits of the product, and include a call to action at the end that specifically tells people to purchase the product.

TIP: At this point, the most important thing you can do to improve your listing is to learn the art and science of writing good sales copy.

Now the next point...

Editing Images

Your images are another important factor when it comes to your conversion rates. If you have poor images, you're going to have low sales.

So keep these tips in mind:

 Take good pics. If you're selling your own merchandise, or if a dropshipper doesn't have good pics, then invest in a good camera and take your own photos (or hire a photographer to do it for you). Be sure they're crisp and clear, with a minimalist background (preferably white) so that the focus is on the product.

 Take pics from multiple angles. Be sure to take close ups that show every inch of the product.

TIP: If you're taking photos of used or antique merchandise, be sure to take special care to show the flaws in your photos.

 Edit the pics. You can use image editing tools such as Photoshop.com, Gimp.org (a free alternative), or even web-based tools such as pixlr.com.

 Show videos too. This works especially well when you can demonstrate how a product works.

Next...

Increasing Conversions

The three things we've talked about so far (good images, good titles and good descriptions) are all going to do the heavy lifting when it comes to increasing your conversions.

However, if you check your chosen platform, you'll probably see apps and add-ons that may increase conversions. Generally, these apps and add-ons are going to set you back a few bucks.

Question is, are these add-ons worth it?

Answer: not yet.

If you're just getting your store set up, then focus on polishing those things that will have the GREATEST impact on your conversion rates. And three of those factors are the ones we talked about above: titles, descriptions and photos. (Others include prices and your overall offer.)

Once your store is up and running and you're getting some traffic to it, you can start testing and tracking different parts of your listings to figure out what's really working for you. You'll find out how to do that just a little bit later in this guide.

For now, FOCUS on the core of your business. Get your store set up. Get your products listed. Get a good running start so you can see some results in terms of getting traffic and making money. Then think about those conversion boosting add-ons later.

One more thing...

"Whoa... Listing Products is a Lot of Work!"

Now as you've been reading this section, it may have occurred to you that listing products actually requires a bit of work. Even if you're doing it the easy way – such as using Shopify, AliExpress dropshipping and the Dropified App—you still need to rewrite product listings in order to generate sales. It's all a bit time-consuming. And that's why now is a good time to determine if you want to do it yourself or outsource this task.

Simply put, it may be a better use of your time to focus on marketing your store, rather than writing descriptions and taking product photos.

So how do you determine if you should do it yourself or outsource?

Ask yourself these questions...
What would it cost for you to do it yourself rather than outsource the task?

A lot of people think it's "free" to do a task themselves, but that's not quite true. That's because time is your most valuable resource since it's limited, so you need to figure out the best use of your time.

Let's break it down...

The first thing you need to do is figure out what your time is worth. You can determine this by figuring out what your income goals are for the year, and dividing that by the number of hours you intend to work to achieve those goals. That will give you an idea of how much your time is worth per hour.

Example time...

Let's suppose your goal is to make $100,000 this year. And let's suppose you plan on working about 20 hours per week for 50 weeks. That's 1000 hours this year to achieve your goals.

$100,000 income divided by 1000 hours = your time is worth $100 per hour

That's just an example. Plug in your own income goals and hours worked to determine what your time is worth.
Now that you have a figure, you can determine what it costs to outsource something. For example, let's imagine you look at a set of

listings and determine it would take you 10 hours to create those listings. In this example, if your time was worth $100 per hour, it would cost you $1000 to do this task yourself.

Now all you have to do is figure out how much a freelancer would charge for this same task. If it's $999 or less, then it's cheaper to hire someone else to do it.

But even if it's more expensive to hire someone else, you might still outsource this task. Check out these next questions to ask yourself....

What sort of end result can you produce?

In other words, are you skilled at this task? Or would it be better to hire a professional to get a better result?

As mentioned, your listings can make or break the success of your store, so it's very important that they're as compelling as possible. If you don't have any copywriting chops and your photography skills are lacking, then outsource the task. Even if it costs considerably more to outsource than to do it yourself, remember that this really isn't a cost... it's an investment. And if you hire the right person, it's an investment that's going to pay you back many times.

Next question...

Do you like the task?

Maybe you're good at it. Maybe you'll produce great results. Maybe it's even a high-value task, so you feel like it's worth doing.

But the question is, do you actually LIKE doing it?

If not, outsource it. Because if you really don't like a task, you're likely to drag your heels and slow down your business growth. It's a much better idea to hand it off to a professional who'll get it done fast and get it done well.

If you outsourced your listings, what would you work on instead?

You only have a limited amount of time in a day. That's why you'll want to focus your time on high-value tasks, such as marketing. So when you consider what to outsource, leave the lower-value tasks to freelancers, while you focus on the higher-value tasks.

What is your outsourcing budget?

Chances are, you don't have an unlimited budget, right? So in that case, you need to use the questions above to figure out which tasks you should be outsourcing. Next, rank these tasks in order of which ones you definitely want to outsource, and which ones you'd like to outsource if your budget permits. Then allocate your outsourcing budget accordingly.

Quick Recap

So there you have it – if you want to see good results, then job #1 is to be sure your listings sizzle. That means they should get attention and get people clicking the order button by focusing on the benefits of the product.

Not sure if you can create these sorts of cash-pulling listings? Or maybe you don't have the time? No problem... in that case, you can outsource the task. Check the bonus resource guide to discover places to outsource these sorts of tasks.

Plans, Promotions and Profits

So at this point, we've covered the most important pieces of getting your store set up, such as choosing a good niche, picking a profitable product line, and creating the kind of listings that get prospects swooning over your order button.

Everything else involved in the actual store set up is easy. For example, if you're using Shopify and the Shopified App, you'll find all the documentations and tutorials you need to get your store up and running. It's just a matter of sitting down and doing it (and it's really all pretty easy).

So, we're not going to cover those basics in this manual, as you can find them elsewhere. Instead, what we're now going to do is focus on the next important piece of running a successful store: traffic generation.

Now, you probably have some sense of how to market your store. I mean you've probably read several posts or reports on the topics, watched a few videos, maybe even attended a few webinars. And in just a few minutes, we're going to share with you some of our favorite ways to generate traffic to your store.

But hold up…

Taking the shotgun approach to traffic generation is just going to be a waste of time, money and your advertising arsenal. So before you start driving traffic, it's worth taking the time to create a marketing plan for your business.

Fortunately, you don't have to pull this plan out of thin air. Instead, all you have to do is answer the following questions. In some cases, you'll need to do a little marketing research in order to get good answers, but it's well worth your time.

That's because you're going to get a better understanding of both your target market and your competitors.
Take a look...

Answer These Questions To Develop Your Ad Strategy:

Who is your target market?

The first thing you need to do is get a very clear understanding of who is going to buy your products. This includes understanding the basic market demographics, as that will help you determine the best way to reach them. You'll also want to understand more about their thinking and behavior, as that will help you create ads that really resonate with them.

Here are questions you'll want to answer about your target market:

☐ How old is your target market?
☐ What gender?
☐ Where do they live?
☐ What is their yearly income?
☐ What language do they speak?
☐ What is their education level?
☐ What sort of jobs or careers do they have?
☐ What is their marital status?
☐ Do they have children?
☐ How much money do they spend every year on products in your niche?
☐ What are their problems?
☐ What issues do they have with similar products in your niche?
☐ What motivates your target market?
☐ Does your market use any sort of niche-related jargon?
☐ Does your market buy products like yours online?

... And anything else you can think of to help you better understand your target market.

TIP: Search Google for your audience demographics, such as "dog owner demographics." You'll find reputable sources, such as government sites and marketing research firms who release this data.

TIP: Spend time talking to your marketing on forums, in social media groups and via blog discussions to get a better feel for what they want. You'll also want to survey them to learn more about their demographics and motivation.

How do you intend to reach your target market?

In order to answer this, you need to know where your target market congregates, or what sort of activities they participate in that allows you to get an ad in front of them.

Here are some possibilities:

☐ Paid advertising
☐ Social media
☐ Search engine optimization
☐ Email marketing
☐ Affiliate Program/JVs (joint ventures)

Those are some of the key traffic generation activities, which you'll learn about later in the guide. Other activities include things like blogging, guest blogging, video marketing, viral marketing, contests, free publicity (press releases), offline advertising and similar.

Your job now is to look at what you know about your target market, and determine the BEST ways to reach your market. Go ahead and list as many ways as you can think of, and then rank this list in order of the most effective to least effective ways to reach your target market.

What is your advertising budget?

Naturally, this is going to have a big impact on the type of paid advertising you do. You can create a strategy to reinvest your profits, so that your paid advertising efforts grow naturally over time.

What are your target goals?

Here we're looking at what your income, sales and traffic goals are.

In order to determine this, you may need to work backwards.

Start by determining your income goals.

Figure out how many sales on the frontend and backend you need to achieve in order to meet these income goals. (Which means you need to set a goal for number of customers, and then set a goal for repeat sales for these customers.)

Estimate your conversion rate. (Don't overestimate – depending on the quality of your traffic and your offer, you may only convert 1% or less... at least until you polish your ads, find venues of highly targeted traffic, and engage a two-step marketing process.)

Estimate how much traffic you'll need in order to achieve your traffic and sales goals.

Go ahead and jiggle these numbers a bit to create different scenarios. As you begin to collect actual data once traffic comes in, then you can adjust your estimates to better reflect reality.

Who are your biggest competitors?

These are the people who are selling the exact same products as you (such as other dropshippers in your niche), or those who are selling very similar products to you. You'll want to do research to gather as much information as you can about your competitors. This includes answers to the following questions...

What makes you different and better than these competitors?

As you start advertising in your niche, your prospects are going to wonder why they should buy from you instead of your competitors. You need to develop a brand and an USP (unique selling proposition) that answers this question.

For example, ever notice that you tend to gravitate towards certain brands when you go to the grocery store, even when similar brands would work just as well (and sometimes even at a reduced cost)?

That's the power of a good brand, which is why you'll want to spend some time developing your own brand.

Your USP might center around factors such as:

☐ Exceptional customer service.
☐ Strong guarantee.
☐ Good prices.
☐ Bonus offers.
☐ Unique products not offered anywhere else.
☐ Products that are made in an unusual way.
☐ Products that are "first" in some category.

In order to determine a good USP, you'll need to do two things:

1. Figure out what USPs your competitors are using, because of course you want to position your business in a unique way in the marketplace.

2. Figure out what is important to your prospects. It does you no good to develop a USP (or overall brand) if your prospects and customers don't give a flying fig about it. Your market research will help you determine what is important to your customers.

Once you develop your USP and overall brand, then you can start incorporating it into your advertising campaigns.

What are your strengths and weaknesses?

Simply put, what weaknesses may hamper your marketing and overall business efforts? And what strengths do you possess that are a boon to growing your business?

You'll want to spend some time thinking about this, as knowing your weaknesses in particular will be helpful, as you can make a Plan B to overcome these weaknesses.

For example, if you couldn't write a high-converting advertisement to save your life, then Plan B would be to outsource this to a professional.

How are your competitors reaching the target market?

Simply put, study what your competitors are doing. Sign up for their mailing lists, follow them on social media, search for them online to find out how and where they're advertising. Figure out what's working for them, and then see if you can adapt some of these idea into your overall marketing strategy.

So What's the Plan, Stan?

If you've answered all the above questions thoughtfully and accurately (using research rather than just your gut), then you should have a pretty clear idea of who your market is and how to reach them. So now you need to create a marketing plan based on this data.

NOTE: Don't spread yourself too thin, or you won't get results. Rank your advertising methods in order of most effective to least effective. Then start with your most effective method, create a plan for execution, take action on that plan, and then analyze your results. Once your first method is up and running, then start working on the next advertising method on your list.

In other words, spend a few days or weeks focusing on just one method at a time. Get that ad method up and running before adding another method into the mix. This strategy will help you get better results.

So now let's look at some of the most effective ecommerce traffic-generation methods in more depth...

Promotions: Buying Your Way In Front of Targeted Eyeballs

One of the fastest ways to start bringing targeted, cash-in-hand prospects to your site is via paid advertising. But before you go crazy with your ad budget, you need to figure out your goals, and then design a paid advertising strategy around these goals.

Here are the main questions to ask yourself to help you design your paid advertising strategy:

What is your main advertising goal?

If you want effective advertising, then you need to determine your primary goal before you purchase your first ad.

Here are follow up questions to help you determine your goal:

☐ Do you intend to generate revenue on the frontend (e.g., advertising for growth and monetization)? While making profits on the frontend is ideal, you may find it acceptable to break even on the front end, or even take a loss. This depends on your backend strategy. Which brings us to the next point...

☐ Is your goal to build your customer list and then generate profits on the backend? In other words, are you willing to take a loss on the frontend with the goal of making it up on the backend? If this is your goal, then you need to determine your likely CLV – customer lifetime value -- and go from there.

☐ Are you using it primarily to build your prospect list? In this case, you're using a two-step strategy that involves sending traffic to a lead page rather than to your store.

You get people on your list, and then turn these prospects into cash-paying customers,

☐ Are you using your advertising to build brand recognition?
Take note: while you can and should build your brand, using paid advertising to do it isn't necessarily the most effective way. Plus, ideally your goals should be easily measurable—and brand recognition is more difficult (but not impossible) to measure, as you'll need to do surveys and focus groups to see if your brand-building efforts are working.

TIP: Regardless of whether you're making money on the frontend, breaking even, or taking a loss, you need to figure out how you're going to extract the most profit out of the backend of your business. This means setting up a strategy and a sales funnel for following up with customers to announce sales, promote related items, and generally get them to spend more money with you.
You'll do this primarily via email, in flyers you send with shipments, in strategically placed cross-promotions and upsells on your site and so on. We'll talk more about these sorts of growth strategies later in this guide.

Once you determine your goals, this will help you decide what sort of ads to create and where to place these ads.

TIP: You'll want to experiment with different types of direct-response ads, including:

1.General store ads. These are ads that direct people to the storefront.

2.Specific product ads. Here's where you advertise some of your most popular products – perhaps low-priced products—to turn prospectsquickly into customers. (This strategy will likely get you better results over sending people to the storefront – but test to find out what works for you.)

3. Sale ads. This is where you offer prospects a discount, such as a coupon on their first purchase.

4. Lead page ads. This is where you send people to your lead page to build your list, rather than sending them to a product page.

5. Retargeting. This is where you place ads in front of people for specific products they've previously viewed in your store. So for example, if someone looks at a pair of shoes in your store, then you can show them an ad for those shoes when they're visiting other websites. One popular platform to place this sort of ad is on Facebook.

Now the next step is to determine the exact venues in which to advertise.

Here are popular options:

☐ Facebook advertising. Be sure to narrow your audience by demographics and behavior to ensure your ads are landing in front of targeted prospects. As noted before, you can also use retargeting.

☐ Reddit.com. This is a fairly inexpensive place to test advertising. Be sure to pick a targeted sub-Reddit.

☐ YouTube.com. Here's a good way to reach your market through video ads (which appear before regular videos on the site).

☐ Google and Bing advertising. Here your ads will show up alongside the organic search results. Be sure to pick targeted (narrow) keywords.

Marketplace advertising. Sites like eBay and Amazon let you advertise on their sites, even if you're not selling products through their platforms.

 Third-party services. Some websites exist to bring advertisers and content publishers together. For example, you might check out sites such as BlogAds.com

 Niche sites. These are sites within your own niche where your target market congregates. You can also check if these sites offer opportunities such as email advertising, or ads on their social media channels.

For example, if you're selling dog supplies, then you'd seek out dog training (and similar) websites.

Keep these points in mind as you develop your advertising strategy:

 Focus on one ad venue at a time. Get it up and running, and succeed (or fail) before you purchase ads through another venue.

 Be sure you're placing effective ads. Testing and tracking your ads will help you determine which ads get you the clicks, customers and revenue.

 Request demographics. Find out as much as you can about a website's traffic – who these visitors are and how the site obtained them—before you decided whether to place an ad with the site.

 Start small. Test a venue with a small ad buy. If you get good results, then you can invest more money in a bigger ad buy.

Once you have your paid advertising strategy in place, then you can move onto the next strategy...

Promotions: Optimizing Your Store For the Search Engines

Right at this moment, there are people searching Google, Bing and other search engines for the EXACT products you're selling in your store. Question is, are they going to find your site at the top of the search engines... or your competitors' sites?

If you want to get your store to the top of the search engines, then you need to use SEO (search engine optimization).

This is a two-step process:

Step 1: Determine what your prospects are searching for.
Step 2: Optimize your store and blog for these keywords.

Let's take a closer look at these two steps...

Step 1: Pick Your Keywords

What you're going to want to do for this step is grab a good keyword tool and use it to figure out what words your prospects are typing into the search engines. All you have to do is enter a broad keyword (such as "gardening" or "women's fashion"), and the tool will deliver hundred if not thousands of related keywords

Heads up...

You're not going for the big words, the ones with the most traffic. That's because there are big sites with deep pockets and teams of SEO specialists who darn near work around the clock to corner the market on words like "weight loss" or "women's fashion."

Instead, what you're going to do is locate VERY specific keywords with small to moderate amounts of competition, and then optimize your pages around these keywords. Generally, these keywords will include:

☐ Very specific product names, such as: "Nike men's Revolution 3 shoe."

☐ Very specific produce reviews, such as: "Nike men's Revolution 3 review."

☐ General product searches, such as: "men's running shoes."

☐ Buying-related searches, such as: "buy men's running shoes" or "men's running shoes free shipping."

☐ Information searches, such as: "top men's running shoes."

☐ Location-specific searches, such as "men's running shoes Los Angeles."

The more specific your keywords, the more targeted your audience. For example, if you're selling Nike men's Revolution 3 shoes, and you optimize for buying related searches (e.g., "buy Nike men's Revolution 3 shoes"), you know you're bringing some relatively warm traffic into your site.

So the point is, forget about the broad (vague) and highly competitive keywords. Instead, focus your efforts on highly targeted keywords.

Step 2: Optimize Your Pages

Now that you know what words you're optimizing for, you'll do this in two places:

1. On your product pages. You can put prospects right in front of the products they want to buy.

2. On your blog pages. Here you can post product reviews, product demos, and even "how to" information related to your niche, and then bring traffic in from the search engines by including your keywords in this content.

TIP: Don't stuff your pages with keywords, as the search engines may rap you on the knuckles for it (meaning your page will appear low in the search engine rankings, or maybe not at all, if the search engines think you're spamming). Instead, inject your keywords into your content at a rate of 1% to 2% (meaning your keywords will appear once or twice for every 100 words of content).

Here's a checklist you can use to optimize your product pages. Include your keywords (such as the brand name and type of product) in:

☐ The page title.

HINT: Use 70 characters or less here so that the search engines don't truncate your title.

☐ The page URL.

☐ The H1 tag (the header on the page).

☐ The image alt text.

☐ Image captions.

☐ Image filenames.

☐ Navigation links or other internal links.

☐ Within your product description itself.

☐ Meta description tags, which is the content appearing under your page title in organic search results.

NOTE: Not all search engines use these tags, but it doesn't hurt to include them. Keep the meta description length to 150 characters or less so that search engines don't truncate it.

Then walk through these other points on the checklist to ensure your product pages (and blog pages) are optimized for the search engines:

☐ Keep your focus on your human visitors, not the search engine bots. Write for humans first, and bots second (as long as writing for the bots doesn't diminish the experience for the human visitors).

☐ Make sure you're using a mobile-friendly theme/design.

☐ Be sure your site loads fast.

☐ Create content-rich pages (especially with blog posts, where you have more leeway to expand).

☐ Include synonyms and words related to your keywords. For example, if your keyword includes the word "housebreaking," you might also use words such as "house training," "potty training," and "

☐ Set up related social media pages and link back to your store.

☐ Install social media

☐ Set up review pages on sites like Yelp and Epinions, and link back to your store.

☐ Create an XML sitemap.

☐ Use canonical tags if you have duplicate content (such as similar product descriptions), or avoid the issue altogether by changing the descriptions.

☐ Create original content. Don't use product descriptions from drop shippers. (Not only does original content help you with SEO, it also helps with conversions and sales.)

- ☐ Use redirects for pages that no longer exist.

- ☐ Check your site regularly for errors, such as broken links or scripts that don't work.

- ☐ Offer videos, interactive features and other "rich snippets." These snippets may appear in the search engines, which will have your page standing out from among the text-only pages.

Quick Recap

SEO is your key to ranking well in the search engines, and it doesn't take too much extra time to include keywords in your product pages. As always, however, you may decide to outsource this task to someone else.

For more information about tools to help you optimize your pages for the search engines, be sure to check out the bonus resource document included with this guide.

And now the next advertising method...

Promotions: Success With Social Media Marketing

Social media strategist Amy Jo Martin says,

"Social media is the ultimate equalizer. It gives a voice a platform to anyone willing to engage."

She's right about that. It's like connecting a microphone to a booming speaker on a busy street corner. Anyone who takes the mic is going to get heard. People can't help but stop and pay attention.

Indeed, social media platforms are like springboards for businesses of any size and with any budget. A small business with a good social media strategy can level the playing field with their deep-pocketed competitors.

And that includes you.

So maybe you're up against some stiff competition in your niche. If you carve out a specialized niche, develop a brand, and then engage on social media, you too can level the playing field.

So here's what you need to do:

1. Clarify your goals.
2. Define your target market.
3. Determine which social media platforms make it easiest for you to reach your target marketing and achieve your goals.
4. Create a custom social media strategy.

Let's walk through these steps...

Step 1: Define Your Goals

Before you develop a social media strategy, you need to figure out what your end goal is. That is, how do you intend to use social media to grow your store?

Here are some ideas to get you started:

☐ Generate new leads/build your mailing list.
☐ Create more sales.
☐ Drive traffic.
☐ Build your brand.
☐ Build authority status.
☐ Boost your viral marketing strategy.
☐ Distribute content.
☐ Engage your audience for research purposes.
☐ Create higher conversion rates.
☐ Develop another communication channel (including for customer service purposes).
☐ Lower your marketing costs.
☐ Bolster your other marketing efforts.

While you may enjoy all these benefits of engaging on social media, you need to primarily pick just one goal, and then develop your social media strategy around that one goal.

Next...

Step 2: Define Your Target Market

When it comes to social media, there are two very important reasons for knowing as much about your audience as possible:

1. It helps you determine which social media platforms to focus on. You've probably heard about the old 80/20 rule. That rule says that 20% of your activities generate 80% of the results. So we're going to figure out which social media platforms are likely to provide 80% of your results, and then focus on those platforms.

2. You can connect with your audience better when you know something about them. In other words, you'll be better able to

post content on your social media platforms that really appeals to your audience.

Two good benefits, right?

For the purposes of this particular discussion, we're going to focus on that first benefit: finding out who your audience is, so that you can then figure out the best social media platform(s) to use.

So how do you figure out who your audience is?

If you're thinking you'll just take a look at your crystal ball or look at some tea leaves, I'm gonna nix that idea right now. We're going to be a bit more methodical about this.

This is a two-part process:

Step 1: Do some market research.
Step 2: Profile your market based on this research.

The good news is, you've already completed these steps when you did your initial market research while planning your store. So now you just need to go back to that research, do some more if you find any gaps in what you know about your audience, and then create an audience profile based on their demographics and behavior.

NOTE: If you need extra help with this step, check out the resource mentioned at the end of this chapter.

Once you've created this profile, move to the next step...

Step 3: Determine the Best Platforms

If you really start looking around online, you'll quickly discover that there are hundreds of social media sites. You could immerse yourself in signing up for those sites starting today, and not come up for air for several weeks from now.

But you know what? Most of them are a waste of your time.

So instead of throwing mud at the wall to see what sticks, what you're going to do is choose from the list of the top seven social media sites.

Here they are:

☐ Facebook
☐ YouTube
☐ Twitter
☐ Pinterest
☐ LinkedIn
☐ Google+
☐ Instagram

And how do you choose?

Simple: you use the profiling information you already have on hand about your audience and then compare this to what is known about the audience profiles on the above sites. Then you select and focus on just one or two of the top platforms that best fits your audience demographics and overall business goals.

One way to get this information about the platforms is simply by researching the demographics yourself. You can find some of this information right on each of the social media's sites, typically in the "about" section.

For others, you'll need to do some research using Google or Bing. Be sure that you draw your numbers and research from reputable sources, especially those that conduct their own research (such as PewInternet.org) or those that link to their references.

Step 4: Develop a Social Media Strategy

Now what you need to do is develop an overall social media strategy. Remember, you're going to start with just one or two platforms and focus on them until you start seeing good results.

You've already defined your overall social media goal – that will drive your social media strategy.

Here are questions to ask yourself to help you develop your social media strategy:

☐ What sort of content does your audience seem to respond to the best? (Hint: look at your competitors' social media pages to get ideas.)

☐ What type of content do you need to create for your chosen platforms? (For example, if you're on Instagram, then you need to share pics. If you're on Facebook, you can create and share a wider variety of content.)

☐ How will you integrate your branding into your social media strategy?

☐ How often will you post on your social media accounts? (Hint: Posting at least two or three times weekly is the minimum – you'll likely want to post more often.)

☐ What sort of tools will you use to schedule content and track responses? (See the resource document included with this guide to learn about your options.)

☐ Will you outsource content creation or do it yourself?

☐ How will you engage your audience to produce more likes, comments and shares? (E.G., Asking, "What do you think?" at the end of a post.)

☐ What sort of viral content will you distribute?

How will you integrate your social media campaigns within your store? (For example, you can place social media "like" and "share" buttons next to products as well as below blog posts.)

 How much time will you set aside each day to interact with your audience, respond to their questions, etc.?

What you'll want to do is develop a strategy using the answers to the questions above as a guideline, and then test your strategy. Test content length. Test text versus multimedia. Test out the time of day you post, the day, and how many times you post per week to see which strategy gives you the best reach.

Remember, social media isn't an advertising platform – it's an engagement platform, a place to share content. So while you may post promos from time to time, remember that social media should be a dialogue (rather than a one-way monologue) – so engage and interact accordingly. If you build a relationship with your audience, they'll be much more open to

Quick Recap

Some store owners sign up to every social media platform available and then use a shotgun approach. That's a mistake. Instead, you need to profile your audience first, pick one or two platforms where your audience is most likely to congregate, and then develop a social media strategy that's designed to meet your goals.

The Magic of Building a Big Email List

At this point you have some traffic coming in, and you've developed a strategy to grow that traffic by taking consistent steps every day to generate new traffic. Yay, you!

So here's what's next: you need to start building a mailing list ASAP.

TIP: You should have multiple lists. At a minimum, you should have a customer mailing list (those who've actually purchased something from you) and a prospect mailing list (those who've joined your newsletter list and are still kicking the tires a bit, so to speak).

Sometimes new store owners put this task on the back burner, but that's a big mistake. That's because a well-built and well-cared-for list will become your BIGGEST asset. You own it. It's yours. And you'll quickly discover that a big list will become your biggest source of revenue.

Consider this...

Even if all your traffic sources dried up tomorrow, such as if the search engines dumped your pages or social media changed their rules, you'd still make money as long as you maintained your list.

And even if your inventory was destroyed in a freak act of nature, you can still make money –any time you want—as long as you maintain your mailing list.

Plus here's something else you'll want to consider...

If you're not building a mailing list, then up to 99% of your traffic is going to come to your store, hit the back button without buying anything, and NEVER return. Ever.

Oh sure, some of these visitors have every intention of returning. Maybe they even bookmark your store. But the moment they leave, they're going to forget about you. Visiting your store again is somewhere on their to-do list below re-grouting the tub. In other words, it ain't gonna happen.

But get these prospects on a mailing list instead, and you can remind them to come back to your store. You can entice them with coupons and other incentives to make that first purchase. And you can build a relationship with them, which will turn them into loyal, lifelong customers.

So what you need to do is make every effort to capture your visitors' email addresses so that you can follow up, close the sale, boost your conversions and grow this valuable asset (your mailing list). Here's how to do it...

Step 1: Get Email Marketing Software

Here you have two choices: you can use a third-party email service provider (ESP), or you can host and manage your own mailing list.

We suggest you use a third-party service. That's because a reputable third-party service works hand-in-hand with ISPs and email providers to ensure your emails land in your subscribers' inboxes. If you took this task on yourself, you'd hardly have time to run your store.

Step 2: Set Up An Autoresponder

Once you've selected a service provider, then follow their documentation to set up your autoresponder. This is quick and should just take a couple minutes.

Once it's set up, you're going to want to load your autoresponder with an initial series of messages to build relationships with your new subscribers and start generating sales.

Let me give you examples of the types of messages you might send out:

☐ Limited-time coupon series. Here you offer new customers a coupon for a discount off their first purchase. You can then send out a series of three to five emails reminding them to take advantage of the offer, plus you can point the towards some of your most popular products.

☐ Informational series. Here's where you send out a "how to" or tips series.

For example, let's suppose you sell grilling supplies. You can send out a series showing people how to grill various meats to perfection, and then promote your grilling supplies from within these emails.

☐ Product series. Here you send out a series of product reviews to showcase your most popular products.

☐ Case studies. If you're selling products that produce some sort of results for people, then you can send out a series of case studies to show how well these products work.

For example, if you're selling gardening supplies, then you can send out case studies for items such as seeds, fertilizers and organic pest control sprays.

In other words, create an initial series to build trust with your new subscribers and generate sales. Then move onto the next step...

Step 3: Create an Incentive to Join

Merely promoting a "free newsletter" isn't going to create any big rush to join your mailing list. That's why you need to give your prospects a GOOD reason to join.

Here are two good reasons:

☐ Give new customers a discount coupon for their first purchase in exchange for joining your list. (E.G., "Join now to get 20% off your first order!")

☐ Offer customers a gift for joining your list. This gift might come in the form of a report, app, video, or other valuable product that's easy for you to distribute automatically. For example, if you sell home improvement equipment, then you might offer a free video series that teaches people how to do common home improvement tasks (such as refinishing kitchen cabinets).
Next...

Step 4: Promote Your Opt-In Form

Now you're ready to start building your list. The next step is to incorporate your opt-in form around your store and website. In every instance, be sure to include the benefits of joining your list, along with a call to action.

Here's where to put your form:

☐ Create a lead page. This is a standalone page whose sole purpose it is to entice prospects to join your mailing list.
Instead of sending traffic to your storefront, you may consider utilizing a two-step marketing strategy and sending traffic to your lead page instead.

☐ Use a lightbox pop-up. You can set this pop-up to appear shortly after people first arrive at your storefront or on a specific product page. This works particularly well if you're offering a discount coupon off their first purchase.

Insert forms on your blog. If you have a blog, then there are several places you can either insert opt-in forms directly, or insert links to your lead page.

Specifically:

-The sidebar of your blog.
-The header or footer of your blog.
-In the navigation menu (link to your lead page).
-At the end of articles.
-Direct calls to action within the articles themselves.

 Install an exit redirect. Don't let exiting visitors leave without giving them one last chance to join your list.

 On your other platforms. Be sure to put opt-in forms or links to your lead pages on your social media platforms, as well as in any content you distribute (such as videos on YouTube).

Quick Recap

You now have a step-by-step blueprint in hand for getting your email capture system up and running.

So what's next?

Now you need to learn how to tap into the gold that lays hidden in your mailing list. That's what's next.

Read on...

Mining The Gold That Lays Hidden In Your Mailing List

You're getting some traffic. (Yay!) You're building a list of prospective buyers. (Yay!) And now you need to engage that list to build relationships and start generating sales. So read on to discover the best practices, strategies and secrets to helping you mine the gold that lays hidden in your mailing list...

Create a Strategy

First things first – you need to develop an email marketing strategy.

See, a lot of store owners think of an idea for an email, create that email, and send it out. But there's no rhyme or reason to their publishing schedule. And if you don't develop a strategy around a specific goal, you end up with poor response rates, unsubscribes and other problems.

So ask yourself these questions as you develop an email marketing strategy:

☐ What are your overall goals for your mailing list?

☐ What sorts of promos do you plan on running, and when?

☐ What kind of content can you send to build relationships? In other words, what sorts of "how to" articles, tips and other informational articles are can you create to inform subscribers (build relationships) and close sales?

For example, if you sell dog supplies, you might write an article about how to leash train a dog who pulls on the leash. Then you might promote a "no pull" collar and leash set within this article.

☐ What sort of holidays would you like to observe with your mailing list? (E.G., If you sell candy, then you're sure to want to send special promos out during Halloween, Christmas and Valentine's Day.)

☐ What sorts of events are relevant to your niche? For example, if you sell clothing, then you'll send out seasonal newsletters. E.G., selling beachwear during the summer months.

TIP: Be sure you know your audience. For example, it does no good to advertise beachwear in July if your audience is in the Southern hemisphere (where it's winter in July).

☐ Are you doing any content swaps with partners? If so, you'll need to plan their mailings into your publishing calendar.

☐ Which products do you want to focus on moving? "All" is not the correct answer here, because you can't promote all your products in your newsletter. (Assuming you have dozens, hundreds or even thousands of products.) That's why you'll want to pick your top products and promote them in your newsletter.

☐ How can you use your newsletter to promote these products? NOTE: Generally, a series of emails about a product creates more sales than sending out a single email about a product.

Once you answer all these questions, then you'll be able to create a publishing calendar so that you know what sort of emails you'll send and when over the next six to twelve months.

In other words, don't just send out an email because it's time to send an email. Instead, send out emails with a specific purpose, such as promoting a new product in your store, promoting a seasonal item, or announcing a sale.

When you have a plan in hand, then move onto these others steps and best practices...

Send Emails Regularly

You can't very well establish a relationship with prospects if you're only contacting them once or twice a month. At a minimum, you need to contact them weekly – you may even find better conversions by contacting them multiple times per week.

Brush Up On Copywriting

Copywriting (the art and science of writing great sales copy) is the #1 skill you can develop to start getting better results from your email marketing efforts. That's because great copy will ensure you create subject lines that get the clicks, and emails that keep people engaged and clicking on your links.

Here are tips for writing better copy:

❑ Create benefit-driven copy. Your readers are always wondering, "What's in it for me?" So when you're describing a product, don't just describe the features (parts) of the product. Instead, let prospects know what those features do for the prospect. In other words, let readers know the benefits of the product.

E.G., The titanium casing protects your laptop and all your valuable pictures, videos and documents against damage and loss if you ever drop this machine.

*Note: The "titanium casing" is the feature. The line above
then explains the benefit of this feature.*

Arouse curiosity. An email subject line that arouses curiosity will get people opening your email. An email that arouses curiosity will keep people reading. And sprinkling a little curiosity near the call to action will get the click.

 Push emotional buttons. People need a little emotional push to move towards the order button.

For example, let's say you're selling clothing. Your promo for a black party dress might include something such as, "You'll be all the envy of your friends when they see you in this jaw-dropping little black number...

 Provide proof. An easy way to do this is by providing testimonials and reviews from satisfied customers. These testimonials can cover the products themselves, as well as issues such as shipping times and your customer care.

Next...

Use Responsive Templates

A lot of your prospects are likely reading your email on their mobile devices. That's why you want to make sure that it's formatted well. If you're sending HTML emails, then use a responsive design to ensure a good reading experience across devices.

Segment Your List

One way to improve the response rate of your mailing list is to segment it into targeted sections. That way, you can send highly targeted content and promos to each segment.

At a minimum, you should split your list into prospects (those who haven't purchased anything yet) and customers. But you'll enjoy higher conversions if you can segment your list in other ways.

For example, let's suppose you sell clothing. You'll make more sales if you can segment your list into those who are interested in women's clothing versus those who are interested in purchasing men's clothing.

Here are other ideas for list segmentation:

◻ Segment your list according to list behavior, such as those who clicked on a link or those who didn't open your last email.

◻ Segment by basic demographics, such as age, gender and location (where relevant).

◻ Segment according to lead magnet. That is, offer different incentives for joining your list, and then segment accordingly.

◻ Segment your list according to what people purchase. This makes it easier for you to send targeted offers to create backend sales.

◻ Segment according to where the traffic originated. For example, if a segment of your population came from Facebook, then you might refer to a special offer for Facebook Fans only.

Those are just a few ideas to get you started. Many major email service providers make it easy to segment your list, so use this feature and track whether segmenting boosts your conversion rates.

Next...

Track and Test

Many major email service providers give you the basic tools you need to track and test your campaigns—use them! You can then do things such as:

▢ Test different subject lines to see which ones get you a higher open rate.

▢ Test different products and offers.

▢ Test specific things within your email such as the opener or calls to action to see which gives you the best conversion rates/most clicks.

Be sure to just test ONE thing at a time in your emails. That way, you know that if there is a difference between conversion rates, it's because of that one factor you tested.

For example, let's imagine you're testing email subject lines. What you'll do is create two emails that are EXACTLY the same, except for the subject line. Then you'll send those two emails out at exactly the same time, so that time of the day doesn't become a factor that influences conversions.

NOTE: An email service provider with built-in testing tools will handle all the details automatically, including splitting your list randomly and then sending the emails out at the same time to these random segments of your list.

So now that you have a good idea of how to boost your email conversion rates, you'll want to take a look at this checklist...

Use This Checklist

There are plenty of pieces and parts to remember when you're sending out campaigns and emails.

Use this checklist to be sure you cover all your bases...

Goals

Do you have a well-defined goal for this email?

Did you plan your content and pitch around this goal?

Is this email part of a series? If not, would your goal be better served by creating a series?

From Field

Have you selected a recognizable "From" field?

Is your "From" field brandable?

NOTE: Pick your "From" field carefully, as you do not want to change it once you've decided on it.

Subject Line

Does your subject line give your prospect a good reason to open the email? (Does it grab their attention?)

Does the subject line include a benefit?

Does the subject line arouse curiosity, where possible?

Is your subject line short so that the email client doesn't truncate it?

Email Content

Does your email immediately engage readers with a direct benefit, a story, an intriguing question, a startling statistic or similar item?

Is your email reader-oriented? (Hint: You should use words like "you" and "yours" much more often than self-centered words like "I" or "me.")

Is your email structured in a way to naturally lead people to your offer at the end?

Do you answer the question, "What's in it for me?" by offering a list of benefits?

Do you include high-quality product photos in the email?

Do you provide a strong call to action alongside a link?

Do you give your readers a good reason to click on the link now? (E.G., a time-limited discount offer is a good way to create a sense of urgency.)

Email Formatting

Are you using a responsive email design?

Did you test your email across devices to be sure it looks good?

Did you proofread your email?

Did you test the email's spam score?

Testing

Did you switch your email's testing tools on so that you can test and track this email?

Are you only testing one factor at a time, while holding all other variables constant?

Segmenting And Follow Up

Are you sending highly targeted emails to different segments of your list?

Do you have another email with a different subject line ready to send to people who didn't open the current email?

Do you have another email ready to send to people who open the current email, but don't click on the link?

Do you have another email ready to send to people who open and click on the link, but don't purchase the offer?

Quick Recap

Building your list is only part of the battle. If you want to make money with your list, you need to develop a relationship with them by sending them a combination of good content and product promos. The key here is to treat your list like you would your best friend, by staying in touch regularly, only recommending the best products to them, and focusing on solving their problems.

Now let's look at another way to grow your store...

Affiliates and Partners and Referrals...

Some of the best and warmest traffic you'll ever get is when someone else directly refers traffic to you. Because think about it – we are much more likely to do something when someone we know, like and trusts tells us to do it (versus if we see an advertisement about it). That's why you'll want to consider installing an affiliate program or other partner referral program.

But heads up – this traffic and list-building strategy may not work for all store owners. The #1 thing you need to consider is whether you have the margins to be able to share a cut of the profits with affiliates.

TIP: Check with other store owners in your niche are offering affiliate programs. If no one else is doing it, there may be a reason – the margins just aren't there.

If you're a dropshipper, then chances are the margins are too small. The exception is if you are in a very specialized or high-end niche where you're not competing on price with others.

If you're selling your own products, then you'll need to consider whether your pricing strategy supports affiliates. If you raise your prices, will you still maintain a good conversion rate? If not, will the extra sales make up for the loss of profits? (Keep in mind that backend sales are a big part of it.) Can you offer enough of an incentive (in the form of a big commission) to attract top affiliates to sell your wares?

Still another thing to consider is whether your business model supports breaking even or even taking a loss on the frontend by giving affiliates most of the profits. In this case, your goal is to build a list of buyers and make the bulk of your profits on the backend.

You'll need to consider all these issues carefully. If you do decide to set up a partner referral program, you'll pick from these options:

1. Set up an affiliate program. Generally, you'll offer a commission on every sale referred to you by affiliates. Depending on what you're selling, commissions on physical goods usually range from between 5% to 25%, with most products right around the 10% range.

2. Set up a customer referral program, where customers (or even prospects) get rewards (instead of commissions) for referring their friends.

Let's look at these two options separately

Set Up An Affiliate Program

Before you set up an affiliate program, you need to get your email list up and running. That's because an affiliate program isn't going to be very profitable for you, unless you are already marketing to your customers on the backend.

In other words, your margins are going to be small on the frontend, so your affiliate program is only going to be a big success you have a plan for monetizing the backend of your business. This may include:

☐ Sending promos via email on the backend. (This is the most important thing you can do to increase sales on the backend.)
☐ Sending promos along with shipments.
☐ Adding upsells on the order form.
☐ Adding promos on the thank you/confirmation page.

So let's talk about how to get your affiliate program set up...

Step 1: Decide On Commissions

Here's the simple truth: the higher your commissions, the more high-quality affiliates you'll attract. That's why selling a high-end product with a generous commission is going to help you build a better affiliate program than selling low-priced items that offer affiliates very little incentive to promote.

Step 2: Install Your Affiliate Program

Depending on your platform, you may be able to use an app or plugin to create your affiliate program. For example, if you're using Shopify, then all you have to do is pick from one of several good affiliate apps in their app store.

On some platforms (like Amazon), your affiliate program is already built in, though you won't have any control over the program, nor will you even be able to contact affiliates. (That's a big disadvantage of using these sorts of platforms.)

Next...

Step 3: Create Marketing Materials

Your next step is to make it easy for your affiliates to join your program and start promoting immediately. You can do this by creating "cut and paste" type promos and graphics for your affiliates to use. These materials may include:

☐ A variety of graphics, including banner ads and smaller graphical squares.

☐ Short text ads for platforms such as pay per click advertising.

☐ Short promos for social media platforms like Twitter.

☐ Longer promos for other social media and blogs.

☐ Articles that are part content, part promo for blogs and newsletters.

Coupons.

 Videos.

 Rebrandable reports.

 Apps.

In other words, create a variety of both text and multimedia content for a variety of platforms. Then be sure to ask your affiliates what else they need or want to promote.

Step 4: Recruit Partners

Now you need to build your affiliate team.

You can do this by:

 Including a link in your store where you advertise for affiliates.

 Let your social media followers, blog visitors and newsletter subscribers know you're looking for affiliates.

 Directly advertise your affiliate program on affiliate-related websites.

 Seek out the top affiliates in your niche and contact them directly to join your affiliate program. Basically, anyone who is already working in your niche is a good candidate to become an affiliate, including:

-Other product vendors or service providers in your niche.
-Those with big platforms, including big blogs, social media platforms, forums, well-trafficked sites, and newsletters.

-Those who are actively working as affiliates in the niche, including those who are currently selling your competitors' products.

Once you start building your team, then move onto the next step...

Step 5: Motivate Partners

If you are on a platform where you have control of your affiliates, then you'll want to stay in touch with them on a weekly basis and motivate them to promote. You can send out weekly emails with the following kinds of content:

☐ Coupons for affiliates to distribute.

☐ Announcements about upcoming promos.

☐ Announcements about new products.

☐ Showcasing popular products.

☐ Announcing affiliate contests.

☐ Providing new marketing materials for affiliates.

☐ Highlighting how well other affiliates are doing (along with tips of how they're doing it).

And anything else that will motivate your affiliates.

Note: Recruiting and motivating affiliates isn't something you do once and then never again. These two steps are an ongoing process, something you should be doing every single week. If you want your affiliate program to grow, then work on both recruiting new affiliates and motiving the entire team on a consistent basis.

Now let's take a quick look at the other method for getting referral traffic...

Set Up a Rewards Program

If you don't have the margins needed to offer cash commissions to your affiliates, then you may consider setting up a rewards program instead. This is where you offer people – often your existing customers and prospects—gifts for referring customers to your store.

Note: You can offer a direct reward for every referral. Alternatively, you can offer "points" for referrals, which your customers can then exchange for gifts. The more points they accumulate, the better gift they'll receive.

Now whether you're offering direct gifts for each referral or you're working on a points system, you'll want to think outside the box. Specifically, consider what type of gifts you can offer that have a high value to customers, yet actually are a low-cost and easy-to-deliver item for you.

Here are some ideas:

☐ Discounts on future purchases.

☐ Gift cards for your store.

☐ Free products from your store.

☐ Discounts or free products from your marketing partners' stores. For example, if you sell wedding supplies such as bridesmaid gifts, tiaras, decorations and the like, then you may offer discounts with a marketing partner who caters to the same niche but doesn't sell the same sort of products.
(E.G., a jeweler, a bridal gown store, etc.)

◻ Related digital products, such as apps, videos, reports or even access to live events such as webinars. For example, if you're selling bodybuilding supplements and equipment, you might offer a training video or a meal-planning app.

◻ Related services. For example, if you're selling weight-loss goods, you might offer a free consultation to help design a custom meal plan and training program.

You get the idea. Point is, try to come up with rewards that your prospects and customers will really value, yet they won't bankrupt you.

No Cash Incentives Or Rewards? No Problem...

If you don't have much in the way to offer in terms of cash or gifts for referrals, there are two other ways to get referrals:

1. Joint ventures.
2. Viral traffic.

A joint venture is when you team up with other marketers in your niche for mutual gain. Go back to the example above – if you sell wedding favors and accessories, then you might team up with someone who sells bridal gowns. That way you can help each other without competing with one another.

How do you help each other? Simple: by co-promoting each other all through your respective sales funnels.

For example, you can swap endorsements and promos in the following places:

◻ Emails to both prospects and customers.
◻ Social media.
◻ Blogs.
◻ On thank you/confirmation pages.

In content you co-create, such as lead magnets (reports, videos, etc.).

You might even do events together, such as holding a live webinar where you promote both of your stores at the end.

The second way to bring in referral traffic is by creating and launching viral content on social media. This traffic won't be as warm as other sorts of traffic, because your prospects will be passing around the content that happens to include a promo, rather than specifically telling their friends to buy from you.

Here's a classic example of viral content: BlendTec and their famous "Will it blend?" videos on YouTube. This campaign was launched over a decade ago, and it still continues to draw views.

Here's how: This company regularly shows off their product line of blenders by creating humorous, eyebrow-raising videos where they blend items such as iPhones. The videos show how well the product works, but the videos also go viral since they're unconventional.

Need more inspiration for viral content? Check out Facebook pages and YouTube videos in your niche to see what's hot. This content may include videos, memes, infographics, and more.

Quick Recap

Two good ways to start getting partner traffic is by starting an affiliate program and offering a rewards program. You'll need to check your margins and your business model to see if these types of programs make good financial sense for you. If not, then two additional ways to get traffic is by partnering with other people in your niche and launching viral content. These two methods are good additions to your marketing arsenal regardless of whether you have an affiliate or rewards program in place.

Customer Care... or Customer Swear?

So at this point traffic is coming in at a nice clip. You're building your list. You're making sales. Life is good!

But don't kick your feet up and lace your fingers behind your head just yet. That's because you still have to put in place one very important piece: a system for handling customer care.

Plenty of store owners don't give too much thought to this piece of their business, but that's a huge mistake. That's because your prospects and customers will judge you based largely on the quality of your customer service.

If you provide outstanding service (consistently), your customers' loyalty to you will grow. All is well. Business will be good.

On the other hand, you're going to be feeling a world of hurt if you can't or won't provide a good customer experience. Bad customer service can destroy your reputation and destroy your business.

You don't have to look far for proof. Just look at any business on Yelp with a low rating, and chances are the customer service is what tanked the rating. Reviewers will even say the products are great, but they'll never return because of the way they were treated.

And you know what? People who have a good experience may or may not tell anyone. But people who have a BAD experience tell everyone. They go on social media. They go on review sites. They tell their friends. You can say "bye, bye business" if it happens to you.

Maybe you've even seen this in your own life. You shop at a store loyally for months... and then one bad customer service experience turns you away from the store FOREVER. And you tell your friends about it.

Because think about it...

You customers can probably get your products elsewhere, no problem. But they can't get good customer service everywhere, so they'll develop strong brand loyalty to anyone who treats them well. You need to step up and be the person who treats your customers like gold, makes them feel valued, and makes them feel special.

So how do you provide this sort of top-notch customer service?

Take a look at these tips and best practices...

Consider Outsourcing

One common complaint from customers is that companies don't answer questions in a timely manner. If you're trying to handle customer service yourself, then you're likely going to get the same sorts of complaints (and lose customers because of it). That's why you'll want to consider outsourcing this task to a competent customer care representative (or team).

A few points to keep in mind:

▢ Train your staff. Even if the staff has a lot of experience with customer care, you want to be sure the staff handles inquiries quickly and professionally.

▢ Provide answers to common questions. This saves your customer care team time, plus provides a uniform experience for customers.

▢ Be sure your customer care team speaks and writes English well. You don't want your customers to get frustrated because of misunderstandings and language troubles.

Next...

Use a Good Help Desk

A good help desk will keep tickets organized, allow you to install a live chat option, and ensure customer's emails don't fall through the cracks.

Cut Down on Questions

One way to make your customer service experience better is by making it easy for people to find what they need without taking the extra step of contacting customer service.

You do this in the following ways:

☐ Provide a FAQ and other documentation. Let people know what to expect regarding common issues such as types of payment accepted, shipping costs, delivery estimates and similar issues. Where applicable, provide text and video documentation on how to use a product (such as user's manuals).

☐ Consider installing an artificial intelligence bot. A good bot will cut down on questions going through the customer service desk.

Let Customers Know What to Expect

When customers contact your business via email (or help desk), you don't want them to feel like their question dropped into a black hole. Post your business hours and time zone clearly on your site, along with an estimate of when you'll get back to them. You can post this same information in an autoresponder that you send whenever someone contact you.

Which brings us to the next point...

Handle Inquiries Fast

If a prospect has a credit card out but wants to ask a quick question before ordering, they're not going to wait around forever. If you take too long to answer the question, they're going to find a competitor instead.

Point is, handle all inquiries as quickly as possible. Whenever possible, offer live chat support to provide instant answers. Help desk inquiries should take a couple hours to answer at most – but you're more likely to save the sale if you can answer more quickly.

Provide Care Across Channels

With the advent of social media, customer service is no longer contained to your site. If you have a Facebook Page, Twitter account or any other social media platform, be sure to check your pages and messages daily. That's because some people will send their questions through these platforms rather than fiddling around on your site.

Make Customers Feel Valued

In addition to promptly providing useful answers, you can provide a good customer experience simply by making customers feel valued. Thank them for their question. Thank them for their business. Let them know how much you appreciate them. And if you mess up, make it up to them (such as by offering discounts or free products).

Keep Customers In The Loop

Once customers hit the order button, you'll want to let them know what is happening every step of the way. So send out emails (these can be automated) that let customers know important information such as when the order is likely to ship, as well as information such as a tracking number once it ships.

Likewise, keep customers in the loop whenever they lodge an inquiry at your help desk. For example, if you're refunding a purchase, let them know when the return arrives, let them know when you've credited their account, and give them an estimate of when the credit will appear on their credit card statement.

Offer Live Support

As mentioned above, offering live chat is one way to provide fast answers to customers. You'll also want to consider offering phone support, as some people want to talk to a "real person" rather than handling everything by email.

Stay Calm

Sometimes people who're having a bad day will attempt to take it out on you and your customer service staff. They'll berate you, they'll use bad language, they may lie about what's going on, they may insult you personally, they may even threaten you.

Take a deep breath. If you feel your blood pressure going up or you feel like firing off a nasty email to "get back" at them, that's a sign you need to take a step back. Once you feel your emotions settle, then and only then should you answer the inquiry.

Remember, one bad customer service exchange can end up on social media and destroy your reputation. So be sure you're always handling customer inquiries promptly, calmly, professionally.

TIP: This doesn't mean you need to let customers abuse you. If a customer is abusing you or your staff, handle what needs to be handled (such as a refund), and then block the customer from your store.

Be Sure Your Site Runs Well

You'll want to regularly check your site to be sure you don't have broken links, inaccurate information, or order forms that don't work. Most people who encounter these problems will simply walk away without telling you (and you can bet they won't be back).

In short, good customer care starts with providing a good onsite experience and a user-friendly site.

Plan For Heavy Loads

There are going to be certain times when your customer service load is going to be a bit heavier than usual. You'll need to compensate for these high-traffic times by bringing on more staff. It's best if you anticipate these periods ahead of time, rather than scrambling and falling behind under a deluge of customer-service inquiries.

Here are some times when you can expect heavier loads:

☐ During sales.

☐ After big sales. (You'll get return inquiries, questions about how to use the product, etc.)

☐ During affiliate contests.

☐ Whenever you've created extra traffic, such as through a new ad campaign or even a viral campaign.

☐ When your store gets mentioned by a prominent influence in your niche, such as by the media, by a well-trafficked blog, etc.

☐ Before gift-giving holidays such as Christmas.

☐ During niche-relevant events or seasons. (E.G., if you sell smoking-cessation aids, you'll see an uptick around New Years as people set their resolutions to quit.)

You'll want to think about your own niche, and when you're likely to see an uptick in traffic and sales.

Anticipate Questions

No matter what kind of store you own, there are certain types of questions that are bound to come up repeatedly. You'll want to have these questions on file, along with a copy and paste template of how to answer them. This saves both you and your customer staff time, plus it ensures multiple customer service reps are handling inquiries in the same way.

NOTE: Some of these questions are suitable for inclusion in your FAQ document. Keep in mind that even if they appear in a FAQ, a few people will still inquire via your help desk.

Here are the inquiries and questions you're likely to receive:

☐ What payment methods do you accept? (Or specific questions such as "Do you accept PayPal?")

☐ How quickly do you process orders?

☐ When can I expect my order to arrive?

☐ I didn't get a receipt/tracking number – can you resend this information?

☐ What is your return policy?

☐ What is your guarantee policy/warranty?

☐ How do use a coupon?

☐ How do I use a gift card?

☐ Do you have any coupons/Groupons available?

☐ Do you have any upcoming sales?

☐ How do I use the product/is there an owner's manual available?

☐ Can I order a replacement part?

☐ This item didn't work – what are my options?

☐ How do I start a return?

☐ Do I need to pay for postage on a return?

☐ Is there a restocking fee?

☐ Do you have telephone number where I can speak directly to a real person?

☐ I'm furious about _____. How do I contact the manager or owner?

☐ Did my order go through?

☐ Where is my order?

☐ Do this, or I'm going to leave a bad review...

NOTE: Some people have such bad customer service experiences that they start out every inquiry with a threat. Stay level-headed and answer these inquiries
cheerfully and promptly.

☐ I just hit the order button and realized I ordered the wrong item/size/color/etc. – how can I correct this before it ships?

☐ I keep getting an error when I try to _____. What now?

I asked for a refund 7 days ago and haven't heard anything back. Are you trying to rip me off?

 Can you flush a dead fish down the toilet? (That probably has nothing to do with your business, but you can bet you're going to get some off the wall questions sometimes – so be sure to handle them in a polite, professional way!)

Quick Recap

Again, don't overlook this piece of your business. Handling customer concerns can make or break a burgeoning business. People have been known to organize boycotts over bad customer service. Don't let this happen to you – use the tips and best practices above to provide great service and start building a good reputation in your niche.

Once everything is running smoothly, then you're going to want to turn an eye towards future growth.

That's what's next, so read on...

Sell Lots, Scale Up... Smile Big

If you put into place everything we've talked about so far, you're going to have mailing lists, traffic logs, sales numbers and revenue to make you smile. But if you want to grin from ear to ear every day, then your next task is to focus on growing your business.

Here's how...

Reinvest Your Profits

Once you start pulling in a few bucks with your store, you're going to be tempted to spend those profits. If you have a day job, you'll want to quit. If you've got something to prove to everyone who said it couldn't be done, you might be tempted to blow those initial profits on something nice, like a new car or exotic vacation.

Hold up...

If you spend your profits as fast as you make them, then you're going to end up with a store whose growth plateaus and goes stagnant. Not good, right?

So here's what you do instead: invest your profits to grow your store.

Initially, you may want to invest ALL your profits right back into your store. As your store grows, you may scale back the amount you reinvest, such as 75%.... then 50%... then whatever number keeps your store growing.

Here are good places to reinvest:

☐ Outsourcing (from creating product listings to customer care).
☐ Advertising.

◻ Conversion optimization.

Which brings us to the next point...
Test and Track Relentlessly

Many store owners throw good money after bad. Or they spend a lot of effort doing things that aren't bringing in the profits. Not intentionally of course, but rather because they simply don't know what's working in their store.

Don't do that. If you want to grow your store as quickly as possible, then you need to find out what's REALLY working.

You need to track and test:

◻ Emails (subject lines, offers, sales copy).
◻ Product pages (sales copy, photos, prices, etc.).
◻ Order forms.
◻ Upsells.
◻ Backend offers.
◻ Ad campaigns.

Basically, you need to find out what products your audience wants, what prices get them cracking open their wallets, and what words (sales copy) boosts conversions.

Next...

Build a Brand

When you first start advertising, you're going to be relying on direct-response ads to get sales going. You send an email to your list, you make sales. You start up a Facebook ad campaign, you makes sales. Your affiliates run a promo, you make sales.

This is all good stuff. But you also want to create top of mind awareness in your prospects and customers, so that they think of your store even when they don't have one of your advertisements sitting right in front of them.

How do you achieve this? The answer: by developing and building a strong brand.

Keep in mind that a brand isn't just about a logo and a slogan. Instead, it's about creating a specific feeling in your prospects and customers. Your brand logo and slogan support this feeling.

For example, the luxury watchmaker Rolex isn't going to position itself on having durable watches or good value watches or even exceptionally good timekeepers. Instead, Rolex is all about wealth, power and sophistication. And that's embodied in the crown logo and the related slogan, "A crown for every achievement."

So the question is, how do your customers feel when they shop at your store? How do you want them to feel?

Once you figure this out, then you can create a logo, color scheme and slogan (unique selling proposition) that support this brand.
Then you can integrate this brand fully into your marketing, including:

☐ Creating a web design around the brand.
☐ Sending emails that showcase this brand.
☐ Creating advertisements with your branding infused.
☐ Using social media photos that highlight the brand.
☐ Creating content that supports the brand.
☐ Training customer service staff to handle inquiries in a way that supports the brand.

You get the idea – basically, your brand should drive your activities. And it should be everywhere, so that your customers and prospects have a consistent, uniform experience whether they are browsing your store or interacting on your social media pages.

End result? You'll create the top of mind awareness that drives long-term growth.

Here's another idea...

Let Competitors Do the Heavy Lifting

Your top competitors already invest a lot of time and money to figure out what works. You can take advantage of their hard work by swiping some of their ideas. Of course you should still test these ideas for yourself, but they're great stating points.

For example, check out what your competitors are heavily promoting – chances are, those are the products that are selling the best for them. Likewise, look for products that are specifically designated as top sellers, as well as those with lots of reviews. If they're selling well for your competitors, they'll probably sell well for you too.

Of course don't stop your "spying" with products. Sign up for your competitors' newsletters. Join their social media pages. Check out their blogs. All of these activities will give you clues about what works in terms of content and promotions. You can then use these ideas as inspiration for creating your own content and campaigns.

NOTE: You'll notice I said "inspiration" – you're not copying, you're modeling what works.

Next...

Focus On The 20%

The 80/20 rule says that 20% of some specific thing is going to produce 80% of the results. This is true in your business too.

For example:

20% of your customers are going to create 80% of revenue.
 20% of your affiliates are going to produce 80% of affiliate sales.
 20% of products are going to produce 80% of your profits.

And so on.

Your job as a store owner is to identify the 20% that produces the 80% of results, and then invest the bulk of your time and money on managing and improving that 20%.

Next...

Email Those Who Abandon Carts

One big source of lost sales happens when people abandon their carts and then forget to come back and complete their purchase. You can save the sale simply by sending an email to those who abandon their carts. In fact, you can do this automatically on many platforms by adding an extension or app. It's one simple step that can produce big profits for you over the long term.

Here's a related idea...

Use Retargeting

Sometimes people get really excited about your store and products. They might even bookmark your site with the full intention of coming back. But once they leave your site, they forget. And there goes the sale.

That's where retargeting comes in. Retargeting lets you remind your prospects about a specific product (or your entire store) by putting an ad in front of them when they are visiting other sites. So if someone looks at a dog toy in your store and then leaves, you can retarget by showing them an ad for that exact same dog toy when they're on another site like Facebook. It's a great way to close the sale, even if the prospect didn't join your list.

You can get started with retargeting (AKA remarketing) using Facebook's ad platform, or by using sites that offer retargeting services, such as www.adroll.com.

Next...

Personalize Promos

One of the keys to generating profit on the backend is to offer products that are highly related to the product your customer just purchased. That's why you'll want to personalize your backend and cross-selling promos to the extent that's possible.

Now if you're using a platform like Amazon, then Amazon does this for you automatically. Just look at their product pages and the pages they show you after a sale, and you'll see recommendations for products that are very similar or complimentary to what you just purchased.

For example, if you purchase a bird feeder, Amazon is likely to recommend that you also purchase bird seed.

If you purchase a cap for your favorite sports team, you'll get recommendations for shirts, jackets, mugs and other team merchandise.

You can do the same thing on your platform by using apps, plugins or extensions that show related products. You can show these related products as a cross-sell during the ordering process, directly after the order is complete, and you can even include a note in the thank-you email.

TIP: Some of the bigger autoresponder services let you create automation rules, where you can add people to specific lists or send specific emails based on their behavior. So if someone purchases a certain product, you can automatically send them an email about a related offer.
And finally...

Consider Your Exit Strategy

At this point you're still reading up about how to start and grow your store. So why on earth are we talking about an exit strategy already?

Simple: because your exit strategy is going to heavily impact your future profits.

A lot of store owners don't give an exit strategy any thought until the point when they actually do want to exit the business. But if you want to maximize profits, you need to run your store with your exit strategy already in mind.

For example, let's suppose you decide to create an online store that's built around the branding of your name. You spend years building the brand, growing the store, and living a comfortable life as a result.

Then one day you decide to retire. You decide to sell the store to the highest bidder. And since it's a very profitable store, you expect to see a bidding war and a big sale price.

Except the problem is, YOU have become an integral part of the store. You're the face of the store. Your name is the brand. When you step away, a very valuable part of the business is gone. Your store simply isn't going to be as valuable, especially if you decide that you don't want some stranger to continue to use your name and likeness to promote the store.

See the problem?

So that's why you need to develop your exit strategy today. Think about how you intend to leave the business.

For example:

☐ Sell the store to a stranger.

- Sell the store to a current employee.
- Sell the store to a family member.
- Sell the store to a friend.
- Sell the store to an existing partner.
- Give the store away to a friend or family member.
- Close the door and walk away.
- Drop dead and let someone else worry about it.

(That's not a comprehensive list – but it gets you thinking...)

Once you know what you're going to do, then build your store with your exit strategy in mind. In other words, design your store for a smooth and profitable exit.

For example:

- Create a brand that's easy to transfer.
- Create a business model that's easy for someone else to take over.
- Create ad campaigns that the new store owner can replicate.

Another thing you'll want to consider is whether you have family that need to be taken care of in the event of your untimely demise. If you'd like your store to support your family after you're gone, then you need to write down everything you do on a daily basis to grow your store— and start training your family members ASAP.

Now let's wrap things up...

Conclusion: This Is The Beginning

So this is it...

You're at the end of the guide.

But this is exciting, because it means you're now at the beginning of your journey as an online store owner.

You've probably got a few visions of your store floating through your head. You can just imagine the pride you'll feel when your store is up and running – and it's yours, all yours. You can imagine telling your friends and family about it. And oh yes, you can imagine the money that will come in – and what it will feel like to quit your job to become and head chief of a burgeoning online store.

Exciting, right? This is the stuff that keeps you up late at night and sends you flying out of bed in the morning. This is the stuff that gives you an adrenaline jolt that's better than anything you've experienced.

Now here's the thing...

None of this is going to happen on its own. The working elves aren't going to do your market research tonight while you sleep. They're not going to build your store. They're not going to set up your list or start driving traffic.

All of that is on you. Not that you have to do it all yourself, of course – you can outsource. But you're the one who needs to put the ball in motion. And the sooner you do that, the sooner you'll start reaping the rewards.

So this is where it starts.

You have a complete step-by-step plan in your hand.

This includes:

☐ Deciding if running a store is a good fit for you.
☐ Choosing your niche and product line.
☐ Selecting the right selling platform.
☐ Building your mailing list.
☐ Driving targeted traffic to your site.
☐ Growing your store over the long term.

These are all the steps you just discovered inside this manual. This a proven strategy that we and countless others have used to start and grow profitable online stores.

And now you can put this strategy to work for you too!

And that's not all. You also have a workbook to help you walk through the entire process. We've made it as easy as possible for you to start and run your store – ***now it's up to you!***

In short, you have everything you need to start building your dream.

So I suggest you start right now. Go back to the beginning of this manual, and work through the steps of choosing your niche and product line. And do it now, because every step you take today puts you closer to owning the thriving, profitable store you've been dreaming about!

To Your Success!

Accelerated Ecom

How To Profit From The Ecom Side-Hustle

Mindset, Motivation and Money

Targets And Goals Workbook

Targets And Goals Workbook

Introduction

If you're looking to start and run a successful ecommerce store, then you need to pick a good niche, develop an advertising strategy, and plan for growth.

This workbook in conjunction with the main manual will help you accomplish all these goals and more.

Take a look...

Determine If Ecommerce is Right For You

Before you start planning your ecommerce store, you need to ask yourself why you want to run this store.

For example:

⬚ Do you want an e-commerce store because you're looking for a way to make money online?

⬚ Do you want a store because you're looking for a way to turn your passions and hobbies into money in the bank?

⬚ Do you want a store as a supplement to what you're already doing? For example, maybe you already have a dog training site, and now you'd like to create another revenue stream on the site by selling physical products.

⬚ Do you already make goods, and you're looking for an outlet to sell them?

⬚ Did you read about someone else having big success with an online store, and that made you daydream about having your own uber-successful store?

⬚ Does it look like an easy way to make money to you?

⬚ Do you want a store because it seems like a good way to help your niche market?

⬚ Do you want a store because you like the idea of owning something? In other words, do you imagine putting "CEO and store owner" on a business card and impressing friends and strangers alike?

☐ Do you want a store because your brother / sister / friend /colleague said they were starting a store, and your ultra-competitive nature kicked in so you wanted a store too?

☐ Do you want a store because your current online marketing gig isn't working out, and you're pretty sure a store would be a much better business for you?

☐ Do you want a store because you tend to chase bright and shiny things, and this seems awfully bright and shiny today?

Those are just a few questions to get you brainstorming.

But basically, you need to be honest about WHY you want to start up an ecommerce store.

The reason you need to be honest about the "why" is because your answer can make or break your success. If you're ONLY reason for wanting a store is because of the money, then you likely won't have the passion needed to keep going weeks, months or years down the line.

So be sure you have a solid reason for wanting to become a store owner.

Brainstorm and Research Niches

The first step in setting up a store is to pick a profitable niche.

You'll start by brainstorming a list of possibilities by asking yourself these questions:

☐ What are you really good at?

☐ What are your hobbies?

☐ What are your problems?

☐ Where do you like to go on vacation?

☐ What do you like to do on vacation?

☐ What types of things do you like to read?

☐ What sort of sites do you have bookmarked on your computer?

☐ What sort of apps do you have on your phone?

☐ What do you like to watch on TV?

☐ What are your favorite topics of conversation?

☐ What sort of educational or hobby classes would you be interested in taking?

☐ On what topics do people marvel at your knowledge?

☐ What topics have you loved for years (and that you're likely to be interested in for years to come)?

YOUR NOTES:

Now list all the other topics you can think of that interest you.

Okay, so now that you've done some initial brainstorming, I want you to go through the following list and pick out any of these topics that also interest you:

☐ Hiking and camping.

☐ Medical problems, including physical and mental health issues, as well as chronic illness.

☐ Caring for elderly parents.

☐ Antiques, collectibles, jewelry.

☐ Babies, children, family.

☐ Relationships and marriage.

☐ Sports hobbies, including golf, archery, fishing, bowling

☐ Other hobbies, such as car restoration, cooking, dining out

☐ Fashion and beauty.

☐ Anti-aging.

☐ Making money, including online marketing, entrepreneurialism, etc.

☐ General finances, including investing / debt management.

☐ Retirement, including financial security and becoming an ex-pat.

- ☐ Traveling, from backpacking across Europe to living an RV lifestyle.

- ☐ Home remodeling and home improvement.

- ☐ Diets, including vegetarianism, raw food diets, etc.

- ☐ Weight loss.

- ☐ Bodybuilding.

- ☐ Motivation.

- ☐ Productivity and time management.

- ☐ Other self-help (e.g., public speaking, feeling more confident, finding happiness, etc.).

- ☐ Grief and mourning.

- ☐ Bad habits, such as stopping smoking.

- ☐ Pets and animals.

- ☐ Career and job.

- ☐ Music, including learning an instrument or learning how to sing.

- ☐ Languages (e.g., learn French).

- ☐ Self-defense.

☐ Home security.

☐ Computer security.

☐ Stress relief, such as meditation and yoga.

☐ Weddings.

You'll note that many of these are very broad. What you want to do is figure out what sub-topics/niches within these broad markets most interest you.

Your Notes:

Once you've created a list of possibilities, then you need to do your market research to ensure these possible niches are profitable.

Take these steps:

Step 1: Find out what your market is already buying. Here's how:

Search marketplaces.

Simply enter your niche keywords into top marketplaces, and see which products are selling well.

You can search marketplaces such as:

- Amazon.com
- Etsy.com.
- CafePress.com
- Zazzle.com
- Bonanza.com
- eBay.com

Search Google. #

Now go search for your niche keywords in Google or Bing.

Take note of the following:

1. What are the top sites in your niche selling? If several sites in your niche are selling similar products, that's a good sign that the product is popular.

2. What are the top sites in your niche advertising? In some cases, a top site might not directly sell their own products. Instead, they may accept advertisers. Take note of what these advertisers are promoting – if you see similar ads across sites, that's a sign that a product is in demand.

3. What do you see being advertised in the sponsored results?
You'll find these sponsored (paid) ads next to the organic ads in Google or Bing. If you see similar products being advertised across ads, that's a sign that it's something popular in your niche.

Check out print publications.

Here's what you're looking for:

1. See what niche catalogs are selling. In particular, pay attention to what is promoted on the front and back covers. These are the big items that tend to be popular, and those who print catalogs do a lot of research and testing to determine which items to put on the front and back covers.

For example, if you're looking to sell gardening supplies, then check out what the top gardening supply catalogs are positioning as their big sellers.

2. See what's being advertised in niche magazines. Popular magazines (with large circulation numbers) charge a lot to advertise, so advertisers pick their products and offers carefully. Check out the ads scattered through these magazines, as well as the classified ads in the back (where applicable).

Your Notes:

Step 2: Find Out What Your Market Wants

Walk through these three steps:

Eavesdrop on your market.

In other words, simply spend some time listening to your market talk amongst themselves, which can be very revealing.

You can find these discussions in the following places:

☐ On niche blogs (check the comments).
☐ In niche communities, such as Facebook groups or niche forums.
☐ In product reviews on sites like Amazon.

Use keyword tools.
The next step is to enter your niche keywords into a tool such as Keyword Atlas. Then pay attention to the keywords that revolve around specific products and product reviews.

Survey your market. Finally, you can ask your market what they want. One way to do this is by using a tool like SurveyMonkey.com. Another way is to simply open the discussion on a big platform, like in a social media group, in a sort of focus group. Or, preferably, you can do both.

Step 3: Pick a niche.

Ask yourself these questions (and answer them based on your research):

☐ Which niches appear to be the most profitable?

☐ Where can you carve out a niche?

☐ Which niches appeal to you the most?

Choose a Platform

The main course gives you a variety of both hosted and self-hosted selling platforms that you can use to set up your store.

But the question is, which one is right for you?

In order to determine the answer, ask yourself these additional questions to uncover your needs?

What sort of products are you selling? Different platforms have different fees, depending on what you're selling, so you'll need to take that into consideration when determining cost. You'll also need to check the terms of service on each site to be sure that the platform accepts your type of product.
If you're selling something prohibited by other sites (such as firearms), then you'll need to consider selling on your own
site (such as by using WordPress + WooCommerce).

What is your level of technical expertise? If you have low levels of technical expertise and/or you don't intend to outsource the development of your site, then you'll need to stick with third-party, hosted platforms (rather than self- hosted options like WordPress). All you do is pay a monthly
fee, and it's headache free.

Do you intend to stock and fulfill merchandise? If you don't carry inventory, then a dropshipping model is a good option (think Shopify plus the Oberlo App and AliExpress), or you can use a service such as eBay's valet service or Fulfillment by Amazon.

☐ **What is your marketing plan?** It's a good idea to market your store aggressively in order to grow it as quickly as possible.

However, some platforms – such as eBay, Etsy and Amazon –help you with marketing, and you get the benefit of their branding to boost conversions.

☐ **How fast do you expect to grow?** You need to be sure you pick a platform that can grow with you. Consider not only how many products you intend to list, but also what sort of volume you plan on doing. Some options, such as Shopify, let you start with a smaller plan and then upgrade as your business grows.

☐ **What is your budget?** Obviously, this is going to have an impact on your decision. But keep in mind, you don't want to go for an unsuitable option just because it's cheaper, otherwise you may need to start over later at a great cost of time and money.

So go ahead and consider these questions carefully, and then visit each of the recommended platforms inside the resource guide to see which one best meets your needs.

Need a quick overview of these platforms? Check this out:

Use The Platform Checklist/Worksheet

Use this checklist to help you decide which platform is right for you. As you complete your research on each platform, you may want to make additional notes about the pros and cons that are specific to your business model.

WordPress + WooCommerce

Here are the advantages of using WordPress + WooCommerce:

☐ It's a stable, secure platform.

☐ You're in control. It's your store, it's your domain, it's your web hosting.

☐ You don't pay per-transaction fees to the platform. (Only to your credit card processor.)

☐ WordPress and WooCommerce are user-friendly.

☐ WooCommerce is flexible, extendable and adaptable.

List other advantages here that are specific to your business model:

Here are the disadvantages:

☐ WooCommerce paid extensions can add up.

☐ The tech stuff is up to you.

☐ Potentially slow loading times.

☐ There is no telephone support.

List other potential disadvantages here that are specific to your business model:

To learn more about the WordPress platform, go to www.wordpress.org.
To learn more about WooCommerce, go to www.woocommerce.com.

Now let's look at another popular option...

Shopify

Here are the advantages of using Shopify:

☐ It's secure.

☐ It's flexible and scalable.

☐ It's customizable.

☐ Good customer support.

☐ You're in control.

List other advantages here that are specific to your business model:

And here are the disadvantages of using Shopify:

☐ Pricing uncertainty.

☐ Learning curve.

☐ Checkout cannot be customized.

List other disadvantages here that are specific to your business model:

Amazon

Here are the advantages of using Amazon's platform:

☐ Credibility and trust.

☐ Built-in traffic.

☐ Security.

☐ You can use FBA (fulfillment by Amazon).

☐ Amazon takes care of the details, such as collecting taxes.

List other advantages here that are specific to your business model:

Here are the disadvantages of using Amazon's platform:

☐ It's not on your site.

☐ Fees can be high.

☐ Direct competition.

List other disadvantages here that are specific to your business model:

To learn more about Amazon's selling platform, go to: https://sell.amazon.com/

And now let's look at the next platform option...

Etsy

Here are the advantages of selling on Etsy:

☐ Setting up your store is easy.

☐ Etsy sends you some traffic.

☐ Etsy is a trusted brand.

☐ It's a good choice if you're creating handmade items.

List other advantages here that are specific to your business model:

Here are the disadvantages of selling on Etsy:

☐ You have direct competition on the platform.

☐ Fees on low-cost products can be high.

☐ You can lose your own sense of branding.

List other disadvantages here that are specific to your business model:

You can learn more about this platform by going to: https://www.etsy.com/sell
or go to: https://etsy.me/3iAjVEv   (for 20 articles free)

eBay

Here are the advantages of selling on eBay:

⬜ You can sell both used and new merchandise.

⬜ Built-in traffic.

⬜ eBay is a trusted brand.

⬜ Setting up a store and listings are easy.

⬜ You can use the valet service.

List other advantages here that are specific to your business model:

Here are the disadvantages of selling on eBay:

⬜ You have plenty of direct competition on the site.

⬜ Fees can be high, depending on what you're selling.

⬜ Your payment options are limited.

List other disadvantages here that are specific to your business model:

To learn more about selling on eBay, go to http://www.ebay.com/sl/sell.

Create Your Product Listings

Another very important factor in your success is to create a compelling sales description for every product you list.

Now before you write your description, you'll want to profile the product to uncover its main features and benefits.

You can create this profile by answering these questions:

> NOTE: If you outsource your listings to a copywriter, then provide this information to your freelancer.

☐ What is the product?

☐ What does the product do?

☐ What color is it?

☐ What is it made out of?

☐ Who made it? (E.G., brand name?)

☐ What are the features of the product? These are the actual parts of a product.

☐ What are the benefits of the product? This is what the features of a product do for the customer. List as many of these benefits as you can think of.

☐ Who is the product most suited for? When applicable, list who would benefit the most from this product.

☐ What are the potential flaws of the product? And how can you rationalize and overcome these flaws? In other words, raise and handle potential objections to help people make the buying decision.

☐ Does the product require any special care? For example, if you're selling clothing, you would note if it's dry clean only.

☐ What are the product's measurements and size? This includes length, height and even weight.

NOTE: Be sure to list product measurements on clothing even if you've listed the size.

☐ How is this product different from other products on the market? In other words, why should people buy this particular product? What makes it better than the competition?

☐ Are there any discounts or freebies available? This includes things like free shipping, as well as any discounts that may be available.

☐ Are there any bonuses included?

☐ Does the product come with any sort of guarantee? If so, what are the terms of this guarantee? Do customers need to pay return shipping? What is the length of the guarantee? Is it a money-back guarantee, or do you only offer product replacement?

☐ Is there anything else the prospect should know that will help them make the buying decision? Go ahead and list everything that comes to mind, even if it seems trivial.

Now that you've answered all these questions, you can write your product description and incorporate as many relevant details as possible.

Be sure to focus on the benefits of the product and include a call to action at the end that specifically tells people to purchase the product.

Determine If You Should Outsource

From creating product listings to taking care of your customer service inquiries, there are plenty of tasks that could keep you chained to your desk all day long.

That's why you'll want to consider outsourcing some of these tasks.

Answer the following questions to determine if and what you should outsource:

What would it cost for you to do it yourself rather than outsource the task?

A lot of people think it's "free" to do a task themselves, but that's not quite true. That's because time is your most valuable resource since it's limited, so you need to figure out the best use of your time.

What you need to do is determine what your time is worth per hour, and how long it will take you to complete a task. Then check to see if a professional can do it at a lower cost.

But even if it's more expensive to hire someone else, you might still outsource this task.

What sort of end result can you produce?

In other words, are you skilled at this task? Or would it be better to hire a professional to get a better result?

Next question...

Do you like the task?

Maybe you're good at it. Maybe you'll produce great results. Maybe it's even a high-value task, so you feel like it's worth doing.

But the question is, do you actually LIKE doing it?

If not, outsource it. Because if you really don't like a task, you're likely to drag your heels and slow down your business growth. It's a much better idea to hand it off to a professional who'll get it done fast and get it done well.

If you outsourced your listings, what would you work on instead?

You only have a limited amount of time in a day. That's why you'll want to focus your time on high-value tasks, such as marketing. So when you consider what to outsource, leave the lower-value tasks to freelancers, while you focus on the higher-value tasks.

What is your outsourcing budget?

Chances are, you don't have an unlimited budget, right? So in that case, you need to use the questions above to figure out which tasks you should be outsourcing. Next, rank these tasks in order of which ones you definitely want to outsource, and which ones you'd like to outsource if your budget permits. Then allocate your outsourcing budget accordingly.

Your Notes:

Develop An Advertising Strategy

Before you start promoting your store, you need to develop an overall strategy. Use the answers to these questions to help you develop this strategy...

Who is your target market?
Here are questions you'll want to answer about your target market:

⬜ How old is your target market?
⬜ What gender?
⬜ Where do they live?
⬜ What is their yearly income?
⬜ What language do they speak?
⬜ What is their education level?
⬜ What sort of jobs or careers do they have?
⬜ What is their marital status?
⬜ Do they have children?
⬜ How much money do they spend every year on products in your niche?
⬜ What are their problems?
⬜ What issues do they have with similar products?
⬜ What motivates your target market?
⬜ Does your market use any sort of niche-related jargon?
⬜ Does your market buy products like yours online?

... And anything else you can think of to help you better understand your target market.

Your Notes:

How do you intend to reach your target market?

In order to answer this, you need to know where your target market congregates, or what sort of activities they participate in that allows you to get an ad in front of them. Here are some possibilities:

☐ Paid advertising
☐ Social media
☐ Search engine optimization
☐ Email marketing
☐ Affiliate Program/JVs (joint ventures)

What is your advertising budget?

Naturally, this is going to have a big impact on the type of paid advertising you do. You can create a strategy to reinvest your profits, so that your paid advertising efforts grow naturally over time.

What are your target goals?

Define your goals in terms of income, sales and traffic. Then estimate your conversion rate and determine how much traffic you'll need to meet your sales goals.

Who are your biggest competitors?

These are the people who are selling the exact same products as you (such as other dropshippers in your niche), or those who are selling very similar products to you. You'll want to do research to gather as much information as you can about your competitors.

This includes answers to the following questions...
What makes you different and better than these competitors?

As you start advertising in your niche, your prospects are going to wonder why they should buy from you instead of your competitors. You need to develop a brand and an USP (unique selling proposition) that answers this question.

In order to determine a good USP, you'll need to do two things:

1. Figure out what USPs your competitors are using, because of course you want to position your business in a unique way in the marketplace.

2. Figure out what is important to your prospects. It does you no good to develop a USP (or overall brand) if your prospects and customers don't give a flying fig about it. Your market research will help you determine what is important to your customers.

Once you develop your USP and overall brand, then you can start incorporating it into your advertising campaigns.

What are your strengths and weaknesses?

Simply put, what weaknesses may hamper your marketing and overall business efforts? And what strengths do you possess that are a boon to growing your business?

You'll want to spend some time thinking about this, as knowing your weaknesses in particular will be helpful, as you can make a Plan B to overcome these weaknesses.

Your Notes:

How are your competitors reaching the target market?

Simply put, study what your competitors are doing. Sign up for their mailing lists, follow them on social media, search for them online to find out how and where they're advertising. Figure out what's working for them, and then see if you can adapt some of these idea into your overall marketing strategy.

What is your main advertising goal?

If you want effective advertising, then you need to determine your primary goal before you purchase your first ad. Here are follow up questions to help you determine your goal:

☐ Do you intend to generate revenue on the frontend (e.g., advertising for growth and monetization)?

☐ Is your goal to build your customer list and then generate profits on the backend?

☐ Are you using it primarily to build your prospect list?

☐ Are you using your advertising to build brand recognition?

Once you've answered all these questions, then you'll have a good handle on who your customers are, how to reach them, and how to stand out from your competition.

Optimize Your Store (SEO)

Here's a checklist you can use to optimize your product pages for the search engines. Include your keywords (such as the brand name and type of product) in:

☐ The page title.

HINT: Use 70 characters or less here so that the search engines don't truncate your title.

☐ The page URL.

☐ The H1 tag (the header on the page).

☐ The image alt text.

☐ Image captions.

☐ Image filenames.

☐ Navigation links or other internal links.

☐ Within your product description itself.

☐ Meta description tags, which is the content appearing under your page title in organic search results.

NOTE: Not all search engines use these tags, but it doesn't hurt to include them. Keep the meta description length to 150 characters or less so that search engines don't truncate it.

Then walk through these other points on the checklist to ensure your product pages (and blog pages) are optimized for the search engines:

☐ Keep your focus on your human visitors, not the search engine bots. Write for humans first, and bots second (as long as writing for the bots doesn't diminish the experience for the human visitors).

☐ Make sure you're using a mobile-friendly theme/design.

☐ Be sure your site loads fast.

☐ Create content-rich pages (especially with blog posts, where you have more leeway to expand).

☐ Include synonyms and words related to your keywords. For example, if your keyword includes the word "housebreaking," you might also use words such as "house training," "potty training," and "

☐ Set up related social media pages and link back to your store.

☐ Install social media

☐ Set up review pages on sites like Yelp and Epinions, and link back to your store.

☐ Create an XML sitemap.

☐ Use canonical tags if you have duplicate content (such as similar product descriptions) or avoid the issue altogether by changing the descriptions.

☐ Create original content. Don't use product descriptions from dropshippers. (Not only does original content help you with SEO, it also helps with conversions and sales.)

☐ Use redirects for pages that no longer exist.

☐ Check your site regularly for errors, such as broken links or scripts that don't work.

☐ Offer videos, interactive features and other "rich snippets." These snippets may appear in the search engines, which will have your page standing out from among the text-only pages.

Develop a Social Media Strategy

Before you develop a social media strategy, you need to figure out what your end goal is. **That is, how do you intend to use social media to grow your store?**

Here are some ideas to get you started:

⁇ Generate new leads/build your mailing list.
⁇ Create more sales.
⁇ Drive traffic.
⁇ Build your brand.
⁇ Build authority status.
⁇ Boost your viral marketing strategy.
⁇ Distribute content.
⁇ Engage your audience for research purposes.
⁇ Create higher conversion rates.
⁇ Develop another communication channel (including for customer service purposes).
⁇ Lower your marketing costs.
⁇ Bolster your other marketing efforts.

While you may enjoy all these benefits of engaging on social media, you need to primarily pick just one goal, and then develop your social media strategy around that one goal.

Now that you've picked a goal that will drive your overall social media strategy, ask yourself these questions to further develop this strategy:

▢ What sort of content does your audience seem to respond to the best? (Hint: look at your competitors' social media pages to get ideas.)

▢ What type of content do you need to create for your chosen platforms? (For example, if you're on Instagram, then you need to share pics. If you're on Facebook, you can create and share a wider variety of content.)

▢ How will you integrate your branding into your social media strategy?

▢ How often will you post on your social media accounts? (Hint: Posting at least two or three times weekly is the minimum – you'll likely want to post more often.)

▢ What sort of tools will you use to schedule content and track responses? (See the resource document included with this guide to learn about your options.)

▢ Will you outsource content creation or do it yourself?

▢ How will you engage your audience to produce more likes, comments and shares? (E.G., Asking, "What do you think?" at the end of a post.)

▢ What sort of viral content will you distribute?

▢ How will you integrate your social media campaigns within your store? (For example, you can place social media "like" and "share" buttons next to products as well as below blog posts.)

☐ How much time will you set aside each day to interact with your audience, respond to their questions, etc.?

What you'll want to do is develop a strategy using the answers to the questions above as a guideline, and then test your strategy. Test content length. Test text versus multimedia. Test out the time of day you post, the day, and how many times you post per week to see which strategy gives you the best reach.

Your Notes:

Develop An Email Marketing Strategy

Your mailing list is going to become one of your most profitable assets. However, in order to ensure this, you need to develop a solid email marketing strategy.

Use these questions to guide you:

⬜ What are your overall goals for your mailing list?

⬜ What sorts of promos do you plan on running, and when?

⬜ What kind of content can you send to build relationships? In other words, what sorts of "how to" articles, tips and other informational articles are can you create to inform subscribers (build relationships) and close sales?

⬜ What sort of holidays would you like to observe with your mailing list? (E.G., If you sell candy, then you're sure to want to send special promos out during Halloween, Christmas and Valentine's Day.)

⬜ What sorts of events are relevant to your niche? For example, if you sell clothing, then you'll send out seasonal newsletters. E.G., selling beachwear during the summer months.

⬜ Are you doing any content swaps with partners? If so, you'll need to plan their mailings into your publishing calendar.

⬜ Which products do you want to focus on moving? "All" is not the correct answer here, because you can't promote all your products in your newsletter. (Assuming you have dozens, hundreds or even thousands of products.) That's why you'll want to pick your top products and promote them in your newsletter.

⁇ How can you use your newsletter to promote these products?

NOTE: Generally, a series of emails about a product creates more sales than sending out a single email about a product.

Once you answer all these questions, then you'll be able to create a publishing calendar so that you know what sort of emails you'll send and when over the next six to twelve months.

Your Notes:

Use This Email Marketing Checklist

There are plenty of pieces and parts to remember when you're sending out campaigns and emails.

Use this checklist to be sure you cover all your bases...

Goals

Do you have a well-defined goal for this email?

Did you plan your content and pitch around this goal?

Is this email part of a series? If not, would your goal be better served by creating a series?

From Field

Have you selected a recognizable "From" field?
Is your "From" field brandable?

NOTE: Pick your "From" field carefully, as you do not want to change it once you've decided on it.

Subject Line

Does your subject line give your prospect a good reason to open the email? (Does it grab their attention?)

Does the subject line include a benefit?

Does the subject line arouse curiosity, where possible?

Is your subject line short so that the mail client doesn't truncate it?

Email Content

Does your email immediately engage readers with a direct benefit, a story, an intriguing question, a startling statistic or similar item?

Is your email reader-oriented? (Hint: You should use words like "you" and "yours" much more often than self-centered words like "I" or "me.")

Is your email structured in a way to naturally lead people to your offer at the end?

Do you answer the question, "What's in it for me?" by offering a list of benefits?

Do you include high-quality product photos in the email?
Do you provide a strong call to action alongside a link?

Do you give your readers a good reason to click on the link now? (E.G., a time-limited discount offer is a good way to create a sense of urgency.)

Email Formatting

Are you using a responsive email design?

Did you test your email across devices to be sure it looks good?

Did you proofread your email?

Did you test the email's spam score?

Testing

Did you switch your email's testing tools on so that you can test and track this email?

Are you only testing one factor at a time, while holding all other variables constant?

Segmenting And Follow Up

Are you sending highly targeted emails to different segments of your list?

Do you have another email with a different subject line ready to send to people who didn't open the current email?

Do you have another email ready to send to people who open the current email, but don't click on the link?

Do you have another email ready to send to people who open and click on the link, but don't purchase the offer?

Create Customer Service Templates

You're likely to get some of the same questions coming in through your help desk over and over again from customers and prospects. You can save you and your staff time (and create a uniform customer service experience) by creating "copy and paste" template answers for these common questions.

Here are the inquiries and questions you're likely to receive:

⬜ What payment methods do you accept? (Or specific questions such as "Do you accept PayPal?")

⬜ How quickly do you process orders?

⬜ When can I expect my order to arrive?

⬜ I didn't get a receipt/tracking number – can you resend this information?

⬜ What is your return policy?

⬜ What is your guarantee policy/warranty?

⬜ How do use a coupon?

⬜ How do I use a gift card?

⬜ Do you have any coupons/Groupons available?

⬜ Do you have any upcoming sales?

☐ How do I use the product/is there an owner's manual available?

☐ Can I order a replacement part?

☐ This item didn't work – what are my options?

☐ How do I start a return?

☐ Do I need to pay for postage on a return?

☐ Is there a restocking fee?

☐ Do you have telephone number where I can speak directly to a real person?

☐ I'm furious about _____. How do I contact the manager or owner?

☐ Did my order go through?

☐ Where is my order?

☐ Do this, or I'm going to leave a bad review...

*NOTE: Some people have such bad customer service experiences that they start out every inquiry with a
threat. Stay level-headed and answer these inquiries cheerfully and promptly.*

☐ I just hit the order button and realized I ordered the wrong item/size/color/etc. – how can I correct this before it ships?

☐ I keep getting an error when I try to _____. What now?

☐ I asked for a refund 7 days ago and haven't heard anything back. Are you trying to rip me off?

☐ Can you flush a dead fish down the toilet? (That probably has nothing to do with your business, but you can bet you're going to get some off the wall questions sometimes – so be sure to handle them in a polite, professional way!)

Yes, it takes a little time upfront to create template answers for these questions, but it will save you and your staff a LOT of time down the road.

Your Notes: